Bare Naked Truths

Stripping Away the Lies That Derail Your Destiny

Kristin Bonin

Contents

Dedicated to Jacey and Emery.

May you always believe what God says about you and shake off all the rest. I love you!

"I'm trying to strip myself down to my barest essentials so I can figure out where I begin and where the woman the world told me to be begins. I'm going back to the starting line. I want to unlearn all the stuff that made me sick and angry. I don't want to come to the end of my life and discover that I never even knew myself."

—Glennon Doyle Melton

Dear Truth Seeker,

Welcome to Bare Naked Truths! Pull up a chair and sit a spell. I'm so excited to be on this journey with you.

Several years ago God sent me on a pilgrimage of my own to become the woman He created me to be, but something was in the way. Lots of somethings were in the way: lies. Lies that I had obtained at almost every stage of life and built on continuously until I realized, *I don't really like the person I'm becoming. She's judgmental, jealous, bitter, insecure, full of both pride and shame, and lacking joy. She loves Jesus but doesn't really feel loved back.* I felt invisible and began working to be seen.

I began to pray, *Lord, set me free from me!* I'll never forget sitting down to talk with a new friend and opening up about a few insecurities I just couldn't shake. She looked at me and said, "You've believed a lie! You need to ask the Lord to show you the lies that are limiting you."

I'll be honest. My first thought was that she had lost her mind. What was she even talking about? She must've seen the look on my face because she grabbed my hand and said, "Let's pray now." *Lord, would you show Kristin the lie she's been believing that's keeping her from a more intimate relationship with you?* I cleared my head and opened my heart and the word 'insignificant' instantly popped into my mind.

I had believed I was insignificant.

Yes, that's the word! It's exactly how I felt and never put my finger on it. It exhibited in my actions and attitude and filtered to my decisions accordingly. It made perfect sense.

Now, if I were the devil and if I knew one of God's children had a calling on her life to tell people how much they matter, and how full of greatness they are, I'd convince her from a young age that her voice didn't count, that no one cared to listen anyway. Well played Satan, well played.

Here's the thing: you have a call on your life. And there is no calling without resistance. The enemy wants to establish false belief systems that direct our paths, one lie at a time. It's not about what happens to us in this life but what we believe through each experience.

I didn't stop asking the Lord that question: *Will you show me a lie I've believed?* I still ask Him and He still answers and shows me when the wrong voice is whispering in my ear.

I want to be that friend for you. When you're feeling down or disconnected, looked over or less than, I would grab you by the hands if I could and look you in the eye and tell you, "You've believed a lie!" The next 31 days are about uncovering those lies and replacing them with God's truth. It's about undressing, unmasking and unveiling the parts of us that don't belong.

Will you allow me to speak to some false belief systems for a moment?

He doesn't hate you.

He's not mad at you.

He hasn't changed His mind about you and decided He doesn't want you as His child after all.

He hasn't forgotten you.

Please don't listen to the voices that echo in your mind that say you don't measure up and don't have what it takes. Everything written in the Bible says otherwise. The more we know God's truth, the more firmly we are planted in His promises. I invite you to spend a few minutes a day for the next 31 days making room for Him by kicking out the lies that have overextended their welcome and laying it all bare before the Lord.

I pray He speaks to you on the pages of this book and I pray His words change you to the core. Here's to the lies becoming history as we embrace the truth that launches us into our destiny!

Get it girl!
Kristin

"Then you will know the truth, and the truth will set you free."
John 8:32 (NIV)

The Biggest Untruth

"She understood who she was and whose she was."
—Elaine S. Dalton

I'm insignificant.
I'm not enough.
I don't have what it takes.
I'm broken.
I'm unlovable.
I am not safe.
I have no friends.
I am hopeless.

You may know it's there. You may not. It could be a thought you think or a string of them that creep in to taunt you when you least expect it. Either way, they're there and they speak to you. These are lies meant to pull you from your purpose and derail you from your destiny. Every lie we embrace nudges us a little further from the truth.

There is a great danger in believing just any voice because we become what we believe. We can always tell what someone believes on the inside based upon the behavior we see on the outside. What the enemy plants as a thought in our mind can grow roots and become a belief system reaching deep into the heart. From the moment we are born, war is waged on who will own our heart. God desires to shepherd it and Satan desires to shatter it. The enemy speaks in so many ways: through people, experiences, and feelings. The spiritual realm knows no slumber and us Jesus girls are marked.

Oh, but we have good news! We have a battle plan.

Exodus 14:14 (NIV)
"The Lord will fight for you; you need only to be still."

In other words: We're gonna have to hush. Hush our mind, our anxious thoughts, hush our opinions and reactions, and hush every voice that doesn't belong to God. That's right! Not today Satan. Not today.

When we are silent, God can speak. This holy hush helps us cease striving and rest in Him. It can bring calm to the chaos and give space for us to deal with our own inner dynamics. Silence helps us hear better and trust me when I say, we need to hear. We must tie truth to us like the life preserver it is.

God's truth drowns out distractions, defines us, brings answers, and peace. It redirects our focus from our problems to our God. Every day we have a choice to decide who has access to our heart.

Which source of truth are we choosing to engage in? Whose words are we letting saturate our soul?

Isn't it funny the things we expect to hear from God? We spend a lot of time asking Him *what to do* and *where to go*, but God wants to talk to us about so much more. His truth isn't that cheap. We settle for a mere information exchange when He desires for us to be grounded in His words that we seek it and speak it. Genuine truth changes *what we believe* and *who we are.*

So, what do you believe? Do you honestly believe that you are beautiful to Him and have a purpose that is outrageously significant? Or is there a lie that's blocking you from that reality?

And who exactly are you? If God had to describe you in one word, which one would He choose? That's worth stopping to think about.

What if we live our lives by the words God picks for us versus the words that strip us of who we are?

He is truth, His words are truth and truth is our only hope. The only language that God knows how to speak is truth. The truth sets people free (John 8:32). His words shatter lies, bring light to darkness and point us to our promises.

God fulfills His purpose in us when we respond to Him. Not just any response, but when we tune into the word of God and do what He is telling us to do; we become who we are created to be. I want to be very clear, the truth is a person. Not a statement. He *is* truth. He shows up in the middle of our circumstances willing to get messy. What God wants to do in us is more important than what God wants to do for us.

Are you up for it? Will you spend the next 31 days letting God's truth uncover you? Will you allow Him to show you the hidden places of your heart? We've spent enough time flirting with untruths and unbelief; it's time we allow God in so he can have a voice. I can only imagine what He will say to you through your time with Him.

The only way to fight a lie is to walk in truth. Let's get to walking!

Lord,

I pray the next 31 days spent in Your word brings freedom like we've never felt before. With every day, strip away the lies that we've held onto for so long and clothe us with the power of Your truth. May Your words come alive and leap into our hearts. Open our eyes to the things we're believing about You and ourselves. Unsettle our souls until we are walking in Your truth and living by Your words.

I ask that You bless every person reading these devotions to encounter You on these pages. Reveal Yourself to them in ways you never have and empower them to share your love with others. I ask for favor: open doors, blessings, and new perspective of who You are. Help us to remember Your truth is what we need, even when it's not what we want. Open the eyes of our hearts and instill in us wisdom.

Thank You that You listen and respond. What a peace it is to know that the things that matter to us also matter to You.

We love You.
In Jesus' name, Amen.

Day One
Self-Worth

A woman who values herself is a woman who values others.

Psalm 139:13 (ESV)
"For you formed my inward parts; you knitted me together in my mother's womb. I praise you, for I am fearfully and wonderfully made."

There's something so beautiful about the idea of something that has been hand crafted.

The stitching.

The attention to detail.

Time spent gathering the perfect materials.

The beauty of creating something useful, valuable and captivating.

The story behind how it was dreamt up with purpose and placed into existence.

The best creators see the demand before there is ever a supply.

As one who appreciates shopping more than you can imagine, I am always on the hunt for unique and well-made items. I was walking through the store the other day and spotted a chic, but edgy pair of heels that would look more than fabulous paired with some jeans and a semi-dressy top. They were shoes you could dress up or dress down and rock the look either way. Black, open toed, chunky heels with studs and a cute zipper on the side. Can you picture them? They were on point and I wanted them instantly. I started gravitating toward them like they were magnetic; drawing me in like a bug to a light and the sooner I got to them, the sooner they became mine. Thoughts were racing through my head as I gravitated toward them in a ridiculous trot through the shoe department.

Would they have my size?

I can order them if they don't.

Should I wear them home?

Let's go out to eat so I can wear them.

I have to have these shoes!

I grabbed them, hugged them (okay, not really), flipped them upside down and-- game changer-- saw the price. My spunky, fun, trendy new heels were $295.

After I picked my jaw off the floor, I sat them back down and had a new thread of thoughts echoing around in my head:

Gross!

Those shoes are hideous.

I don't even like them.

Get away shoes!

I hurried away like they were diseased and repulsive, wanting nothing to do with them. Who needs chunky heels anyway? So overrated.

Here's the thing: when we view something as unattainable, we discard it and move on. We don't try it on. We don't see ourselves as owners of such an expensive possession. We stop dreaming it forward and start settling for where we're at. We don't see the value in ourselves the way God does.

I'm certain the shoes were worth the money. They were name brand, excellent quality, made of the finest leather, and the details were fun and eye catching. It wasn't that I thought the shoes weren't worth the money; it was that I thought *I* wasn't.

Can you let that sink in for a second?

This is about way more than shoes. This is the story of every person who fails daily to see the breathtaking worth we carry in the kingdom of God. And when I say breathtaking, I mean that literally. When God created us, it took His breath. We are spoken into existence with care, detail and an unyielding purpose. Our creator is well aware of the demand before He makes the supply. We can be both humble and confident, knowing we are hand made by a God who doesn't make mistakes.

Some of the most treasured words the Lord has ever given to women in scripture outline a woman of sophistication, class and the upmost integrity.

Proverbs 31:25-31 (ESV)
"Strength and dignity are her clothing, and she laughs at the time to come. She opens her mouth with wisdom, and the teaching of kindness is on her tongue. She looks well to the ways of her household and does not eat the bread of idleness. Her children rise up and call her blessed; her husband also, and he praises her: "Many women have done excellently, but you surpass them all." Charm is deceitful, and beauty is vain,

but a woman who fears the Lord is to be praised. Give her of the fruit of her hands, and let her works praise her in the gates."

Are you clothed in strength and dignity? If you're anything like me, most days you're just lucky to be clothed in anything other than sweaty gym clothes and a messy bun. Oh, to be a Proverbs 31 girl! I mean, how nice for *her*, whoever *she* is. Who is this woman? I want to meet her! I don't know about you, but most days I wear the smelly gym clothes I worked out in that morning. When I open my mouth, I'm barking out orders to my kids while shoving a bagel down my throat as my children rise up and call me 'bossy' and my husband tells me I forgot to shut the garage. And this is all before 8am. Yet, scripture clearly tells me I am this woman and you are too. It's not about what we have to offer this world, but *who* we have to offer this world. Scripture speaks of who we already are in the process of becoming. Proverbs 31 isn't given to us as a standard of ways to measure up, but an exhaustive list of the greatness that already lies within us. We don't have to feel treasured, we are treasured.

The Bible tells us David was a man after God's own heart, yet he was an adulterous murderer. Abraham had the distinct honor of being called a friend of God, even though he was a controlling, manipulative liar.

Mary, a flawed and imperfect woman gave birth and raised Jesus, the Son of God.

Rahab, a harlot, helped an entire nation claim their promised land and through her came the lineage of the Messiah.

Jacob, whose name meant deceiver, ran from God and died highly favored with blessings to give for generations to come.

One common denominator exists among all the greats and heroes of the Bible: they were not imprisoned by their imperfections. Their story became His story. How much more do we understand His grace and mercy than by a love that extends far beyond every fault and flaw? Men and women of faith are those who embrace God and His truth in ways that change their character and nature. They believe God. They believe in themselves and in the process, they believe in others. I want that. I want to walk in all God has for me- the good, the bad and the ugly, whatever it takes to become the gal He's created me to be. I want to be a woman who fearlessly chases down the destiny I was created for simply because it brings me closer to Him. It's out of our great affection for the Holy One that we ourselves become holy.

Imagine if we walked into our day with three fundamental truths:
God loves me. He is the greatest story ever told and I   was created to tell it.
I'm a part of His story.
You're a part of His story.

If all of the above is true (and it is), then our words count and our actions matter. Make no mistake, something as simple as a smile and some kind words can bring healing and hope. God uses our obedience and takes it further than we could ever imagine. Our daily choices are the process of becoming who God created us to be. Let's walk into every day as a worthy storyteller. Remember, Jesus said, "I came so they may have life" and then He gave us the ability to speak life into people and situations on His behalf. What an honor. What a privilege. What a purpose.

Self-Worth

In a world where you can be anything, what will you be? I hope your answer is 'His.'

Lord,

Thank You for Your love. Today, will You allow me to both receive Your love as well as give it away? You are the creator of all things and Your works are beautiful, well made, and perfect in every way. If we look closely we see You in them. Open our eyes to see Your beauty in everything, including ourselves and others. Don't stop creating us. Create in us pure hearts that long for You. Equip us to speak truth and life. We don't want to just believe in You, we want to believe You. May Your word be set into motion through our lives. Amen.

Day Two
Comparison

———

*Comparison sets us back,
confidence sets us apart.*

———

"Love does not envy" 1 Corinthians 13:4 (NKJV).

Find a woman who is confident and focused on the promises of God for her life and she is unstoppable. She's the kind of girl who celebrates what others are doing without allowing them to diminish her own plans and she doesn't dare to compare the two. She recognizes the beauty in herself and therefore recognizes the beauty in those around her because she has a deep understanding that her assignments are from the Lord. Her acceptance is found in her identity, not in her abilities.

This is the kind of woman we all desire to be. The battleground lies in the pursuit of becoming her. She is feared and doesn't even know it, with an enemy who wants to kill her, steal her destiny, and destroy her ambitions. His strategy is simple: distract her.

There's no faster path to discontentment than by way of comparison. Yet we compare our humble beginnings to the most successful and triumphant life accomplishments of others. We compare ourselves to others, where they live, what they drive, job titles, bank account numbers, and what the world defines as success. We compare ourselves to ourselves: where we are versus where we thought we'd be or desire to be. We compare ourselves to an idea of how something should look. There's no shortage of comparisons. When we begin to judge what God does and does not have for us, we lose sight of the purpose for which God is equipping us. I once read a good Pinterest quote that said, "If it doesn't open, it's not your door."

I can tell you that I've spent many hours of my life I'll never get back again, knocking on a door I was never intended to walk through. And do you know what it did? It did nothing to accomplish my purpose. Taking my gaze off of what God has for me and measuring it against what He has for someone else will do one of two things: make me feel too big or too small. When we fix our eyes on the blessings of others, we lose sight of Jesus.

Hebrews 12:1b-2 (NIV)
    "let us throw off everything that hinders and the sin that so easily entangles. And let us run with perseverance the race marked out for us, fixing our eyes on Jesus, the pioneer and perfecter of faith."

This passage goes on to tell us when we focus on Jesus, we will not grow weary or lose heart. That's a promise if I ever saw one! Fling your Bible open, highlight those scriptures, pray them, and live them out. It can only bring freedom if you do.

Brené Brown tweeted some stellar advice not too long ago: "Stay in your lane. Comparison kills creativity and joy." Truer words have never been spoken.

When we peek in on Rachel and Leah in Genesis 29, we learn how scandalous comparison can be. Not only are these sisters trying to win the heart of the same man, they desire to receive the honor and attention they feel they are entitled to. Hang onto your seats because things are about to get rocky. Let's not read these passages thinking it's a story isolated to "them." Put yourself in one of their places. It doesn't matter which one, just pick Leah or Rachel.

Now, let's read: Genesis 29:30-35 (NIV).

"Jacob made love to Rachel also, and his love for Rachel was greater than his love for Leah. And he worked for Laban another seven years.

When the Lord saw that Leah was not loved, he enabled her to conceive, but Rachel remained childless. Leah became pregnant and gave birth to a son. She named him Reuben, for she said, "It is because the Lord has seen my misery. Surely my husband will love me now."

She conceived again, and when she gave birth to a son she said, "Because the Lord heard that I am not loved, he gave me this one too." So she named him Simeon.

Again she conceived, and when she gave birth to a son she said, "Now at last my husband will become attached to me, because I have borne him three sons." So he was named Levi.

She conceived again, and when she gave birth to a son she said, "This time I will praise the Lord." So she named him Judah. Then she stopped having children."
Genesis 30:1-2 (NIV)

Comparison

"When Rachel saw that she was not bearing Jacob any children, she became jealous of her sister. So she said to Jacob, 'Give me children, or I'll die!' Jacob became angry with her and said, 'Am I in the place of God, who has kept you from having children?'"

This. Is. Spicy. Comparison is not a head issue, it's a heart issue. And if we don't tend to the issues of our hearts they will leak out and bleed all over everyone around us.

Here we have two wives, four kids and a husband in one miserable family because no one feels like they are enough.

Until Jesus is enough, nothing will ever be enough. Leah is bringing the family honor by having children but isn't satisfied because she doesn't have Jacob's attention.

Rachel becomes jealous of what Leah has achieved and neither one of them can appreciate what they do have because they are too focused on what they don't.

One has acceptance, the other has achievement. One is beautiful and the other is fruitful. Leah tried to find her value in a man and Rachel in what she could produce.

Wait. Hit the pause button. Which one are you? Are you fighting for the attention of people when God tells us He chooses the unchosen? Or are you chasing down a dream that isn't yours because someone else has what you think you need?

Why are we so drawn to want what we don't have?

I read this story and so desperately want to sit down with these women and say, "Don't you see it? God loves you so. He desires you. He approves of you. He chooses you." And that's the same thing I'd say to you if I could.

Anytime we tie our value and worth to what other people think about us, we are living for the approval of man and the not approval of God. These girls are absolutely infested with the disease to please, but they are not striving to please God. In their efforts to define their own success, they omitted Him from the equation.

From Leah, the rejected wife, came Judah. From the lineage of Judah, came Jesus. The Savior of the world was birthed from someone unloved, undesired and unseen.

Rachel, the barren one, gave birth to Joseph. He eventually saved an entire nation of people and brought us some of the most powerful words in scripture.

What will you allow God to birth through YOU?

Our journey is our journey. It can't possibly be compared to anyone else. You haven't walked the path I've walked and I haven't lived the life you've lived. God is far too creative. He specializes in all things unique.

You don't fit in? Good! That's part of the plan. The body of Christ works better when we function in our role, rather than all trying to play the same part.

Comparison

The emotional cancer of comparison can cripple us. It can make us believe we'll never measure up. So let's sit on these thoughts together:

Someone else's win is not my defeat.

- Her success is my success. It subtracts nothing from what God has for me.
- God has a never ending supply of love and He has more than enough for me.
- Remember that girl we started out talking about? The one who is confident, focused and unstoppable? Today, be her and don't hold back! You've got it in you.

Lord,

I'm sorry I've dared to compare myself to others. Please forgive me for not being content with what You have given to me. Help me to embrace all that You have for me, knowing that Your blessings are in both what You give and what You withhold.

Day Three
Competition

___

Empowered people, empower people.

___

Philippians 2:5 (HCSB)
"Make your own attitude that of Christ Jesus."

I'll never forget one of the most encouraging phone calls I ever received when I first launched my blog. I had a sweet friend who was also passionate about writing, reach out to celebrate with me. Us writers cheer each other on when we have the guts to hit "post." I was nervous, antsy, and felt very vulnerable. She also had a blog and knew the feeling. She simply called to share the moment with me. It meant the world to have a friend spread some encouragement and support a step of obedience. Before we hung up, she said some words that made my heart sink, but they were words that made me respect her because of how gut level honest she was.

"Kristin, I've got to tell you, I'm a little jealous. Your blog is great and I mean that. It's better than mine."

So many thoughts and questions flooded my mind and all I could say was, "That's not true." And it wasn't. We write about completely different things and I could never speak to

17

the things she does. She's been through things I can't wrap my head around. What God has done for her is powerful and needs to be shared. Yet, I understood her words because I've spoken them too. I've felt it more times than I can count. I consistently fight the thoughts that others are better.

Different? Yes.
Better? No.

There was a very distinct thought I had gathered by the time I hung up the phone: *the word "better" is not in God's vocabulary*...but it's very much in ours.

We keep score, jockey for position, feel like we're getting passed by, and can't seem to keep up. Satan wants us to be sidelined with feelings of inferiority or superiority. What becomes dangerous is when competition moves from being an act to an attitude; when we're driven by the applause of man and not the applause of God.

Hey, I love a little friendly competition. Rest assured, every person who has ever been on a tread mill next to me at the gym has unwittingly been in a race. They have no clue, but my goal is to beat them. Never mind the fact that I intentionally select treadmills next to senior citizens and those who are walking and not sweating. That's irrelevant.

Sure, competition can be harmless but when we lock horns on a regular basis, a simple competitive pounce can turn into a full blown competitive personality.

Have you ever had the friend who had to have exactly what you had and then some? Did you find yourself in a battle of constant one-upmanship? Those relationships aren't fun. And I'd even go as far to say they aren't worth it.

I want my friends to see me as an encourager, not an exasperator.

When we listen in on the story of David and Saul, we notice that one of these men was just living life, doing his thing and the other one began to take notice. Rather than considering David's accomplishments a team win, Saul saw them as a threat.

1 Samuel 18:7-9 (ESV)
"And the women sang to one another as they celebrated, "Saul has struck down his thousands, and David his ten thousands." And Saul was very angry, and this saying displeased him. He said, "They have ascribed to David ten thousands, and to me they have ascribed thousands, and what more can he have but the kingdom?" And Saul eyed David from that day on."

1 Samuel 18:15-16 (ESV)
"And when Saul saw that he had great success, he stood in fearful awe of him. But all Israel and Judah loved David, for he went out and came in before them."

Saul could have easily just owned the blessings God had given him. Maybe God would have increased his territory if he'd chosen to celebrate what the Lord had done through him and his friend, David. After all, the battle is the Lord's and so is the victory. We miss God's power when we don't look back at all He's done through us. Missing His power means missing His promises. Rather than seeing David as a tremendous asset to Saul's kingdom, he saw David as a troublesome threat. And so began his downfall.

When we welcome competitiveness into a relationship, we kill cohesiveness. Those who could be teammates in the faith, lifters of your spirit, shift to become opponents. Why stand toe to toe when we were created to stand side by side? A combative relationship is always a burden, never a blessing. The benefits we get by working on a team are far more rewarding than a personal gain.

What would happen if the goal of our relationships were to be a blessing? We can't compete with those we're busy celebrating. If our focus is to speak life and affirm the ones God places on our path, it leaves no room for insecurity. The days are shorter when we find joy in what God is doing everywhere. Let's live in a world where "better than" doesn't exist.

Say this with me: I have nothing to prove.

Did you know, no two zebras have the same stripe pattern? They are all unique in the way God made them. Even wild dogs have their own personal markings and that's how they identify each other even from quite a distance. We have our own markings too. We have various talents, experiences, and favor in different areas. Competition brings no value to any of us. We are what we are by the grace of God.

Bare Naked Truths

In John 10:10 (NIV), Jesus is teaching the Jews and he tells them, "*I have come that they may have life, and have it to the full.*" In other words, He came so that we could all have the life He intended us to have, one in constant connection with Him. He came so that our circumstances could neither overtake nor define us. He came so that we could know Him for all that He is and introduce Him to everyone we know. He came so that we could live loved and accepted.

I can live in constant competition with others or I can live cherished by God. I choose cherished. Let's empower women to live out their destiny.

Who will you bless today, cherished one?

Lord,

I want to be a woman who empowers others to reach their full potential in You. Give me eyes to see and breath to speak blessings to others. I want to compliment, not compete with them. Teach me how to find joy in celebrating my sisters and use me to speak life into all of those You place around me. Remove "better than" from my vocabulary. Let me be Your mouth piece to honor You with my words. I pray You'll empower me so that I can empower others to bring glory to Your name.

Day Four
Criticism

---

*Man's opinion should be filtered,
not followed.*

---

*"When I walked off the stage after giving a talk, a woman
leader came up to me with a big smile. She touched my arm,
leaned in, and said, "Wow, most of the time I can't understand
your messages at all, but I got so much out of this one. And
thanks for not making any of us feel insecure about our beauty
by wearing that tonight." She gave me a hug with a big "thank
you" and "great job" and walked away. It wasn't until much
later that I realized I had been knifed..."*

*Her comments not only spoiled my night, but they left their
marks for a long time. I still fret and worry about being clear
and accessible when I speak, and I try on outfit after outfit
before I give a talk.*

Jenn Oyama Murphy

It happens to all of us: we are lied about, talked about, or
misunderstood. Either they say it straight to your face or it gets
back to you somehow. It hurts. It stings. But their opinion is not
always your reality. The critics will always be there. Always.
The more we say yes to assignments from God, the louder we'll
hear them screaming, pointing out inadequacies and flaws. It's

22

tempting to become defensive and counter-criticize them back, but nothing productive ever comes from that. I say, don't do it!

If I could meet any person from the Bible, it would be my bud, Nehemiah. He's a crazy, strategic leader, full of wisdom, and every time I read his book I learn something new.

He's wise, compassionate, strong and *greatly opposed.*

Nehemiah 4:1-2 (NIV)
"When Sanballat heard that we were rebuilding the wall, he became angry and was greatly incensed. He ridiculed the Jews, and in the presence of his associates and the army of Samaria, he said, "What are those feeble Jews doing? Will they restore their wall? Will they offer sacrifices? Will they finish in a day? Can they bring the stones back to life from those heaps of rubble—burned as they are?"

He is yelled at, made fun of, questioned, and doubted among other things. Poor Nehemiah! He was just minding his own business, working hard for his Creator. He is hustling and bustling to finish his selfless humanitarian project (that he is doing out of sheer obedience to God) and BAM...his character is attacked, along with his progress. Isn't it about right to be faced with your worst when you're doing your best? It never fails that resistance springs up the moment you begin taking a few steps toward your destiny. You know you're in the game when you're eye to eye with an opponent.

When it comes to progress, you'll often find a problem. They're kind of a package deal. Callings come with critics.

Criticism

Not everything said to us or about us requires a response. Jesus was also verbally attacked, lied about, and subject to large amounts of unfair criticism. Most of the time, he didn't reply. That's something for us to consider.

The opinions, thoughts, and feelings of others should be *filtered* before they are *followed*. The greater the responsebilities you obtain, the more critics you will gather. For that reason alone, we must filter and weigh the words that others say to us and about us.

My husband was telling me about an IVC filter the other day. I had never heard of one of these, but it is a small metal device designed to prevent blood clots from traveling to the lungs. I'm always impressed by the medical advancements I hear about. The filter is placed in the large vein that takes blood to the heart. Its purpose is to catch blood clots and break them down into tiny pieces so that the clot doesn't go to the lungs, which would result in certain death.

The truth about criticism is that it can kill us if we don't filter it. It can kill our passions, hopes, dreams, and God given purpose.

When we come toe to toe with criticism, here are some things to consider as a filtering process:
Who is it coming from? Is this a friend or foe?
What is their motive?
What are their fruits?

Bare Naked Truths

Galatians 5:22-23 (NASB)

"But the fruit of the spirit is love, joy, peace, patience, goodness, kindness, gentleness, faithfulness and self-control; against such things there is no law."

Do their words bring life or death? Are they laced with love and grace or anger and bitterness?

Is this a person you've intentionally stationed to guard the walls of your heart?

Is this person consistent or consistently opinionated?

The Man in the Arena: Theodore Roosevelt

It is not the critic who counts; not the man who points out how the strong man stumbles, or where the doer of deeds could have done them better. The credit belongs to the man who is actually in the arena, whose face is marred by dust and sweat and blood; who strives valiantly; who errs, who comes short again and again, because there is no effort without error and shortcoming; but who does actually strive to do the deeds; who knows great enthusiasms, the great devotions; who spends himself in a worthy cause; who at the best knows in the end the triumph of high achievement, and who at the worst, if he fails, at least fails while daring greatly, so that his place shall never be with those cold and timid souls who neither know victory nor defeat.

———

You get to choose who you listen to. You make those choices, but keep in mind, those choices will make you. Are you going to listen to the crowd or the coach? In Nehemiah's case,

25

they kept hurling insults and trying to get him off his project-his calling-his vision.

He answers them in Nehemiah 6:3-4 (NIV), *"I am carrying on a great project and cannot go down. Why should the work stop while I leave it and go down to you?" Four times they sent me the same message, and each time I gave them the same answer."*

He tells them he will not stop what he's doing to entertain their words. The work is too great to give ear to any voice that intends to cause harm. *He decides he must abandon the lies of his enemies if he's going to accomplish the will of his Father.* This is the same decision we must make.

We have trained our dog to only chew on the things that are intended for her to chew on. When she puts something in her mouth that she's not supposed to, we say, "Leave it!" She will drop what's in her mouth and move on.

For every criticism and idle word designed to take you away from your purpose: Leave it. Remember, that's not for you to chew on.

Lord,

Give me Your words to help me filter criticism. Teach me to love the people who have harsh words against me. Show me when to respond and when to be silent. Help me to ignore them and focus on You. My desire is to please You, lean into Your words and reflect Your love. No word or weapon formed against me shall prosper.

Day Five
Regrets

Your past develops you,
it doesn't define you.

Philippians 3:13 (ESV)

"Brothers, I do not consider that I have made it my own. But one thing I do: forgetting what lies behind and straining forward to what lies ahead, I press on toward the goal for the prize of the upward call of God in Christ Jesus."

Oh how I wish we could part with certain things of the past! Just sweep them under a rug or pretend they never happened.

Failed relationships. Broken hearts. Shattered dreams. Red-faced moments. Bad decisions.

If you've ever found your palm on your face questioning if you could just have a do-over, you understand that sinking feeling of regret. Sometimes I wish I could go back in time and redirect my own steps or even punch myself in the face. Anything to re-write history.

Regrets

Recently my friend was telling me about a trip she took to visit her husband's entire family over a holiday break. They all loaded up in a few vehicles packed with kids and adults and visited a local park to let the kids explore. It's always an adventure when large families venture far from restrooms. They had been there for quite some time and honestly, a momma of three can only hold her bladder so long before the idea of wetting herself becomes a scary reality. The kids were riding down hills and enjoying the nearby creek when she decided to sneak away and take care of business, if you know what I mean! Now, if you've never done anything like this before (and she hadn't), there can be a certain degree of anxiety that comes with relieving yourself in the woods. *Will someone see me? What if I get wet? What do I wipe with? Do I wipe?* So she decided to walk back to the car and do the old duck and cover trick. Mid-stream she realizes that she's not alone. Her father in law is right next to her, putting the kids in the truck beside her. Her father in law! I mean, out of all the people in their tribe at the park that day, any other person would have been less embarrassing. She finished as fast as she could and to this day doesn't know if he saw her or not.

These are the things nightmares are made of. I'm still laughing at her- I mean *with* her, to this day. She laughs about it too, but she's still wishes it never happened.

Finish one of these statements:
I wish I had...
I wish I hadn't...

Bare Naked Truths

As I sit and write these words, I wonder what the thoughts are in your head right now. I would love to hear your stories and where life has taken you. I'd love to share mine. We all have things behind us we wish weren't there. Regrets are steeped in what we have or haven't done and sometimes we need to make the decision to get right with ourselves before we can get right with God.

If we're not careful, our past can hold us captive to our future. We can ask ourselves one of two questions: How did I get here? How do I get where I'm going?

Can you glance at Philippians 3:13 again? These are some of the most encouraging words in all of scripture.

Paul wrote these words from a prison cell and if anyone had a past to tell about, it was him. He was born a Jew, the son of a Pharisee and one of the brightest in his class. He excelled so much that he traveled from Tarsus to Jerusalem (over 350 miles) to study under one of the most well-known Pharisee's, Gamailel. Paul was indoctrinated with Jewish law and customs and somewhere along the way, picked up a disdain for Gentiles. Even though it's entirely possible that at some point in his upbringing, he could have brushed shoulders with Jesus, he managed to grow in hatred toward Christ followers and everything they represented. He took on an intense mission to persecute Christians and was known by all as such.

Regrets. He had many. Referred to as a terrorist, with a goal of exterminating Christians, he could have been defined by his mistakes. His actions could have glued him to his decisions, but he realized something major: The value in regret is what we learn from it.

Some of the most influential world changers among us are fueled by their regrets.

What's behind us isn't so bad when we realize it's there to move us forward. With every regret, comes a lesson learned and lessons learned are a wealth of wisdom.

The enemy will try to pull up our deepest regrets and hold them over our head any and every time we attempt to move forward. He'll remind us of what we've done, what we didn't do and the fact that we can't undo it. His mission is to convince us that not only did we make a mistake, we are one. His voice screams: You're inadequate, incapable, unworthy, unwanted...and God can't use someone like that. If he can tie you to the pain of the past, you'll stay stuck. But your pain can only stop your progress if you allow it.

We don't have to entertain the "I wish" list when Jesus provides other options. When Satan brings us shame, we can slow down and remind ourselves of what God's word says.

I will bless the Lord (Psalm 16:7, ESV)
I can do all things through Christ (Phil 4:13, NIV)
I am a child of God (Galatians 3:26, NIV)
I will not fear (Psalm 118:6, ESV)
All things work together for good (Romans 8:28, ESV)

I'm so thankful that the power of Jesus tells me my future rests in His promises, not my mistakes. My past can destroy me or deploy me. What Satan uses to hold me back, God can use to hurl me forward. Lessons are something we learn from and move on. They make us better, stronger, and wiser. However, if we don't acknowledge the lesson, perhaps we didn't learn it.

I can tell my story just the way it is because it's made me who I am today. God may not be pleased with everything I've done, but He's always pleased with who I am. He restores and redeems every wrong and hurtful thing. So, I will look to my past as a reference point, not a resting point. I must park my heart in the pursuit of Jesus.

Lord,

Would You rip off every label that's ever been placed on me and make me new? Can You take every choice I've ever made and use it for Your glory? I want to see You in the areas of my life that say 'no trespassing.' My life doesn't have to be full of perfection to be full of peace. Thank You, Jesus that You are the one who brings peace.

Day Six
Pain

———

God can use our greatest pain as the guide to our greatest purpose.

———

Romans 5:3-5 (NIV)

"Not only so, but we also glory in our sufferings, because we know that suffering produces persever-ance; perseverance, character; and character, hope. And hope does not put us to shame, because God's love has been poured out into our hearts through the Holy Spirit, who has been given to us."

I'm a sucker for movies with a happy ending. Who doesn't like the feel-good movies? I'd much rather walk away with pep in my step than worried that there's a zombie or vampire behind every bush. I give bonus points for movies with a message. Mix my love for happy endings and my husband's love for sports and we find ourselves on the couch, fully engaged in *Facing The Giants* from time to time.

There's a scene where the coach does a football drill at practice with his team captain, Brock. He blindfolds him and straps another player to his back, has him do the death crawl and challenges him to the 50 yard line in the heat, being guided only by the sound of his voice. Brock works hard, takes breaks and does the best he can but hits a breaking point where he almost stops. His pace slows and you can tell he's ready to give up.

"It hurts, he's too heavy, I can't."

"Keep going, don't quit. You don't quit on me Brock Kelly."

Coach keeps reminding him that he promised to give him all he had and tells him to keep going. Then he starts to count him down.

"20 more steps. 10 more. Don't quit till you don't have anything left in you."

What started as a 50 yard challenge, ended as an end zone completion. He pushed through cramps, shortness of breath, aches and every possible pain. When he takes off his blindfold, he sees that the coach took him through the pain in order to accomplish something he never thought he could. Then coach tells him this:

"You are the most influential player on this team. If you walk around defeated, so will they. Can I count on you?"

I wish I could cement those words in our hearts. Don't quit. Keep going. The reward is far greater than the pain. People are watching you in your weakest moments; show them it can be done. Even when it hurts.

In this broken world, we become broken too. Relationship hurts, financial setbacks, sickness, disease, disappointments and loss tend to break us. Yet, hurting hearts still beat. There's still something in them left to give.

Jesus is very clear in telling us we will face hard times. *"I have told you these things, so that in me you may have peace. In this world you will have trouble. But take heart! I have overcome the world"* John 16:33 (NIV). In other words, we don't have to lie down and take it. We can take it by force. There's no possible way to control the events and circumstances in our lives, no matter how hard we try and trust me, I've tried. What we have complete control over is what we do with our heart once it's been torn. When anxiety leaks in and life is unbearable, we have a tendency to hide.

So many times I've tucked my aching heart under my arms and taken off running from anyone else who could possibly do any more damage to it than what has already been done. That's when I find myself, looking around, with no one in sight but the staunch realization that I don't want to run from the people God has placed in my life. He placed them there for a reason and they are my people. Pain is a beautiful thing when it pushes us into the arms of Jesus.

One of the most powerful prayers we can pray is *Lord, please don't allow my hurting heart to become my hiding heart.*

Can I invite you, can I invite *us*, to find hope in the middle of our most hurtful moments?

Some of the deepest scars to my soul have become a stage for Jesus to be seen. For every person who is overwhelmed with a sinking heart, I want to tell you something. It may be a painful season but we have a peaceful God. He hurts with us. He counts every tear. He cares when it feels like no one else does and He is fiercely protective of us even if we don't see it.

We all desire for Jesus to take us higher and I believe there will be times when He will. But if we can trust Him to go deeper, we will meet him in the depths of our sorrows and discover He's there too.

I remember the first time I ever drove an ATV/four wheeler on my own. We had rented some to drive around at the beach. Before we were allowed to drive them, the man we were renting them from gave us a crash course. Not a bad idea, especially for someone like me! The kind I was driving was operated by a button on the handle that I had to hold down and adjust according to how fast I wanted to go. He said something I still remember, "It's going to hurt your thumb. Okay? It'll hurt. Just keep going."

He was right. It hurt tremendously, but if I stopped, it would have affected all the people behind me and I could have missed something really important on the journey. Sometimes the danger of stopping is greater than pushing through the pain.

I'm so glad Jesus didn't stop. He somehow managed to push through the pain.

When I think about what He endured on His way to the cross, I'm reminded of a man who is no stranger to pain. He was betrayed, forgotten, falsely accused, brutally beaten, mocked, denied, and left to die. He somehow managed to make the very intentional decision to canvas the men and women who were responsible for it all. He looked past the pain they were inflicting to see the pain they were in. He wanted this bad enough to not tap out. Even though by all appearances He was not winning, He didn't give up. Ultimately, that took Him to victory.

Before God reconciles you to others, He has to reconcile you to yourself. The times He's met me at my worst, He's asked me one thing: to give Him that moment. To hold onto Him and not let go and in doing so, know Him more.

Holding onto God when it's easier to hold onto pain is where true healing begins.

"You are the most influential player on this team. If you walk around defeated, so will they. Can I count on you?"
Facing The Giants

Lord,
If anyone can take my heart and make it new, it's You. Everything You've ever allowed me to go through serves a purpose to glorify You. Help me to see past people and define Your purpose. Today, You can have my pain and use it as a stage so that others can see You. Give me strength to keep going and use my circumstances to build my character.

Day Seven
Perspective

Perspective can imprison you

or empower you.

Ruth 3:12 (NIV)

"And now, my daughter, don't be afraid. I will do for you all you ask. All the people of my town know that you are a woman of noble character."

There's a prayer I find myself praying often and in various circumstances that has become a staple prayer I go to on default: *Lord, help me see this the way You do.*

Whether it's dealing with a difficult person, a frustrating situation or simply something I don't understand and I'm tempted to get all huffy and puffy, I'll stop myself and pray this prayer. I used to pray for the Lord to remove the problem or the person until I realized problems and people build character. In fact, the people I admire and respect the most not only have solid integrity but also an eye for spotting when God is at work. They've taught me that character isn't built overnight, but it is built in our perspective.

I have two girls and when they get to picking on each other and things escalate, I always tell them, "Those are silly things that aren't worth fussing about."

Then one day, God said it to me.

Ouch.

I found myself in a very, very difficult season and I didn't like any of the outcomes. The conversations that needed to be had, the friendships God was redefining, the direction He was taking me- I wasn't a fan of any of it. My prayer life sounded more like interrogation time with a whole lot of whining. Have you been there? Maybe you're there now.

I marched myself to the throne of God and pled my case. I presented the problems and all the answers and sat back, waiting for Him to do His thing.

Only, He didn't.

He leaned down and whispered in my ear, "Kristin, the things that make you happy are not necessarily the things that make you healthy."

And that's when it hit me...all of these things were happening for a reason. A very specific purpose. I don't have to like it; I just have to trust it. My goal was a happy heart; His goal was a healthy soul.

When we meet Ruth on the pages of scripture, we learn that she is widowed. Her mother in law, Naomi, gives her permission to return to her family but Ruth chooses to stay by her side. I can't imagine what it must have been like for her to not only lose her husband, but also her dream of having children and building a loving home. All that was comfortable and familiar changed in an instant.

Naomi's reaction is made clear.

Ruth 1:20 (NIV)
"Don't call me Naomi," she told them. "Call me Mara, because the Almighty has made my life very bitter."

This is not a woman who sounds easy to love. If she was going to rename herself, she may have been just as safe with Debbie Downer or Negative Nancy, but she chose bitter. She is clearly struggling with her circumstances and allowing her circumstances to cause a struggle with God.

What happens next is intriguing. It's not what Ruth does, but what she doesn't do that allows us to see her more clearly. She doesn't try to control the situation. We can't find where she counseled Naomi, gave her a pep talk or even coached her into feeling better. She simply stayed loyal and available to her and became compliant with the process. We must remember that the process is part of the promise. Naomi decided to be bitter, Ruth decided to be brave.

She had every right to sit down to coffee with Naomi and talk about how much she would have liked to go back to the way things were, but she didn't. She simply remained where God had her. That sounds hard. So hard. To just be still and trust Him when He's doing a new thing, an unfamiliar thing, a thing I can't understand.

39

Perspective

Anytime the Lord has brought me into a new season, I found myself telling Him, "But I LOVED THAT SEASON! I want to go back. I want *those* people back in my life. I want *that* job. I'd prefer to stay where I'm comfortable." Yet, God loves us entirely too much to leave us in our place of comfort. Maybe it's because our comfort and God's glory do not go hand in hand. This I know is true: The end of one chapter is the beginning of another and adventure awaits!

Ruth 2:2-3 (NIV)

"And Ruth the Moabite said to Naomi, "Let me go to the fields and pick up the leftover grain behind anyone in whose eyes I find favor."

Naomi said to her, "Go ahead, my daughter." So she went out, entered a field and began to glean behind the harvesters. As it turned out, she was working in a field belonging to Boaz, who was from the clan of Elimelek."

It just so happened that out of all the fields, she finds land that belongs to her husband's family. There's two ways she could have processed this.

Man, I have to work all day in the hot sun, surviving off other people's left overs. What has my life come to?
OR
This is no coincidence I ended up in a safe field and found favor. I will embrace this moment, knowing it serves a purpose.

What if we lived each moment like we were meant to be there? Every conversation. Every person along the way. Every experience. What if we ran to them with expectation that we're there for a reason? It might shift our thoughts from a "me" mentality to a "He" mentality.

Can we soak in these thoughts together?
God has not forgotten me.
He works all things together for good.
He has me here for a purpose.
I will embrace today and look for Him.

Ruth could confidently say to Naomi, *"Where you go I will go, and where you stay I will stay. Your people will be my people and your God my God,"* Ruth 1:16 (NIV) because it didn't matter where she was, she knew He was already there. She was not left behind or pushed out, she was placed on purpose. It was never about following a person, only about serving God.

God always has something better waiting for us than what we've left behind. The blessing often comes from the test. It's in the middle of my test where I decide if I'm blessed or burdened. Rather than asking God to fix my problems, I'll ask Him to fix my perspective.

Lord,
Help me see things the way You do. I want to meet You everywhere I go, knowing that You have a divine appointment for me to receive and show Your love. Open my eyes to see Your mighty hand at work. Remind me that Your plans are good. They give me hope and a future. Help me find peace in the process of becoming who You created me to be.

Unwholesome Talk

Those who reserve their words,
preserve their character.

Ephesians 4:29 (NIV)

"Do not let any unwholesome talk come out of your mouths, but only what is helpful for building others up according to their needs, that it may benefit those who listen."

Have you ever said something and instantly wished you could grab those words and put them right back in your mouth as if they were never said? There are so many conversations I wish I could un-have.

I can recall countless words spoken from my mouth that were vicious, mean, uninspiring and just plain ugly. The kind of comments that made me feel sick to my stomach after I said them because I knew they were wrong. Why do our mouths have the potential to get us into so much trouble? And why is it so hard to keep them shut? It's like our opinions just have to fly out or it's going to kill us...or maybe that's just me. If I had only known the power that words held sooner in life, there would be fewer regrets. There are many things I would've left unsaid and even more things I would've spoken boldly, without fear or shame. Words are so precious. They can *inspire, challenge, encourage, affirm* and *bring hope*. In fact, it's the words that God speaks to us that make us who we are. The Bible instructs us to cling to His words (Phil. 2:16). Words can shape us and mold us into being who God created us to be.

They can also stop us dead in our tracks. They can dishonor the character that God is trying to instill in us. They can corrode our heart and steal our joy. The words we choose can bring disappointment and discouragement in full force to our own soul and the lives of others. With a single word, we can build or shatter. I don't know about you, but I don't ever want anything with the word "shatter" attached to my name.

Paul also address's our words in 2 Timothy and he's fairly aggressive about this topic. He's the kind of guy I'd like to hear speak. He's clear, concise and means what he says. Can you imagine sitting in church while he's preaching and he says this:

2 Timothy 2:16 (NIV)
"Avoid godless chatter because those who indulge in it will become more and more ungodly."

Those are the kind of statements that fill the room with nervous laughter and awkward fidgets because we've all run our mouths. If we're brutally honest with ourselves, we all probably do it on a regular basis in various forms. Paul's advice is wise.

Godless words lead to godless assumptions. Godless assumptions lead to godless opinions and godless opinions lead to godless actions. And no one wins.

Unwholesome Talk

Words speak life into people or limit it. I intentionally surround myself with truth tellers because speaking truth is powerful. Godly feedback sharpens our integrity and affirmation launches us into our destiny. We must be careful to not offer our opinions unless they are cemented with God's truth. I want to be a friend that is confident in the truth that my words reflect Jesus. Of course, this means I must ask myself one question. When handling people and navigating difficult conversations, *am I guarding my ego or am I guarding another's heart?* Both can't happen at the same time. Pride must be laid on the altar of sacrifice when it comes to guarding the hearts of others. We can speak out of pride or humility, but they are not the same voice. I can make their heart a priority or I can just make a point. One has a lasting impact and the other just has a moment of satisfaction.

The words we choose tend to say a lot about us. Have you ever heard the old saying, *"What Sally says about Susie says more of Sally than it does Susie?"* It's true. It's wise to do a word check from time to time. What am I saying? Why am I saying it? Where is it coming from? *Discontent? Insecurity? Fear?* All words have a source. *"What you say flows from what is in your heart"* Luke 6:45 (NLT). If we'll trace our words back, we may find that there's a vacancy, a job opening for Jesus. Help wanted, please. Sometimes those are the most precious moments, letting Him in to take a look. He never leaves things the way He found them. He loves us too much.

We know we are loved because He *says* we are. It's the kind of love that convinces us we matter. When we share His love, we convince others they matter. Who has the Lord given you to speak into? He places people around us constantly-family, friends, and co-workers- to encourage, give godly counsel, correct, and offer candid feedback. Oh, how honest feedback can sting! Some of the hardest words I've ever had to swallow brought me to a season of growth. Excuse me while I set my pride aside! Yes words can hurt, but they unlock the truth that sets the world free.

"There is a time for everything...a time to be silent and a time to speak" (Ecclesiastes 3:1).

I remember going to lunch with a friend who was upset with me. I'm sure I had said or done something to merit the conversation we were having. There was a point when I felt it crossed the line from attacking something I did to attacking who I was. After reaching in my soul and picking my heart up off the ground, I was preparing to fire back multiple words that would surely put her in her place. They were really good too. My mom always told me I should have been a lawyer. I was ready to defend myself. Only, that's not what God wanted me to do. These words flooded my mind: Will I find more satisfaction in being right or righteous? In this particular situation, she just needed to be heard. The more I listened, the more I realized I had failed her expectations. I just couldn't dedicate the time she needed in a close-knit friendship. Firing back would have made it messy and hurtful. God was calling me to love her, the best I could. As I was listening to her voice, I was also listening to His "Give what you can and give the rest to me."

Sure, we can listen with the intent to respond or we can listen with the intent to...hear. If we set aside the notion that we need to win the argument or solve the problem, our relationships are strengthened and so is our character. There are times when "no words" are the best option. When we're quiet, God can speak.

Let's make our words count. Choose them wisely. Hand-pick them. Craft them. Ask the Holy Spirit to breathe on them so that they are powerful and effective. And remember, *those who hold their tongue, are held in higher esteem.* May our words be chock-full of His.

Lord,

I will take the words I speak seriously. Reveal Your truth to me and empower me to use them in speech and action. Teach me to pause and think about what I'm saying. I want to speak Your words. They ignite fire and passion to all who hear.

Day Nine
Rejection

_____

What people cast aside,
God keeps close.

_____

Judges 11:1-3 (NIV)

"Jephthah the Gileadite was a mighty warrior. His father was Gilead; his mother was a prostitute. Gilead's wife also bore him sons, and when they were grown up, they drove Jephthah away. "You are not going to get any inheritance in our family," they said, "because you are the son of another woman." So Jephthah fled from his brothers and settled in the land of Tob, where a gang of scoundrels gathered around him and followed him."

Sent away. Cast aside. Completely unwanted. *Have you ever felt it?*

It's the feeling of trying out for the team and not making it. Like being the girl that wasn't asked to the dance, or interviewing for your dream job and being told, "No, thank you." It's the emotion that can cause us to question if we're even in the will of God at all. We've all had that dreadful, sinking feeling in our heart. It seems to come partnered with a certain fear that our dreams might be going down with it. It's not a good feeling and it comes with question marks, lots of them:

Do you really have a plan for me?
Have I completely missed your calling?
Where do I fit in? Did I do something wrong?
Is there anything inside of me you CAN use?
Why am I constantly overlooked?

We can question ourselves into a corner and then feel like we've been put into a spiritual "time out." I've done it more times than I care to admit. All the while, God is patiently waiting by the sideline, ready to answer; just waiting to be heard.

Jephthah appears doomed from conception with a mom who had no interest in him. Add brothers who told him he didn't belong and dismissed him, he had nowhere to go. Just like that. They chose their inheritance over their brother. The very ones that were supposed to love him the most, cared the least. I wish scripture told us about his reaction. What did he think? How did he feel? Where was God in all of this? I often wonder if the men and women in the Bible trusted the Lord in their most difficult times. I hope he knew that even though he was disposable to them, he was invaluable to God.

I hope you know that too. What feels like the ridicule of rejection can actually be the sweetness of God's love and protection. When people fail us, God will not.

When others scream *No*, His love is still there.
Maybe we aren't ready.

Maybe they aren't the right friend.

Maybe that job would've been the worst experience of your life.

Maybe you lived through something horrendous and the sheer fact you're still alive is proof that God's love is chasing you down.

All hope is not lost.

A "no" to our heart is an opportunity to welcome a "know" from God; to know Him more intimately. Sometimes we just need to know in the depth of our being that even if every human on the face of the earth doesn't see value in us, God's love will sustain us. Rejection is painful but it is not permanent. God will allow our soul to ache if it means we find Him in our despair. He desires to be the one we run to. The times in my life I've felt the most pushed aside, God was pursuing me and instilling purpose. We must dare to hurt if we are to be truly healed.

In Matthew 22, the Sadducees and Pharisees were relentlessly questioning Jesus and challenging not only His authority, but His identity. People questioned who He was, what He had to say and every move He made. He always had an accuser and faced incredibly painful betrayals. Can you relate to that? Those who respond to mighty callings will also have to respond to mighty oppositions.

So he asked them point blank, *"What do you think about the Christ? Whose Son is He?"* This was almost identical to the question Jesus asked His disciples in Matthew 16:13-15 (NIV) *"Who do you, say that I am?"* Jesus confronted the ones *against* him as well as the ones *for* him with the need to decide who He was.

"*...and from that day on no one dared to ask Him any more questions.*" Matthew 22:46 (NIV)

The Pharisees needed to be put in their place and the disciples needed the reminder. The same is true for us. When we question God, we need one of the two. If you're anything like me, you often need both.

When our hearts are hurting, we are faced with a question: Who do I say He is? *Is He my Savior? The one I can trust? Is He the one who opens and closes doors for me and always has my best interest at heart? Is the Lord of heaven and earth also the Lord of my circumstances?* We live in a perfectly imperfect world full of perfectly imperfect people.

The thing about imperfect people is that we can hurt each other in the worst ways. We fail, attempt to fix things ourselves, beat ourselves up, and feel really guilty when we can't tie things up in a pretty bow. The prick of others' words and actions can leave us in a puddle of pain.

Hurt people, hurt people. Rejected people, reject people. Inconsiderate people don't consider people. Chances are, you've been on the receiving end. The good news is: God's power flows from our most powerless moments. He is completely aware of our hearts and desires to be the complete Lord of them. He will never reject us, He's not even capable. He tells us in Matthew 11:28, "*Come to Me, all you who labor and are heavy laden, and I will give you rest*" (NKJV). In other words, we don't have to strive for the acceptance our hearts so desperately need. It's already there. We just have to come to Him.

Jephtahs story didn't end with being sent away.

Judges 11:4-6 (NIV)

'Sometime later, when the Ammonites were fighting against Israel, the elders of Gilead went to get Jephthah from the land of Tob. 'Come,' they said, 'be our commander, so we can fight the Ammonites.'"

There came a day when the men of the town realized how valuable of an asset he was and went and found him, asking him to come back and be their commander. The story goes on that the Lord helped him with a victory. He remained faithful to God and God remained faithful to him.

Here is a prayer challenge for today. Perhaps instead of questioning our present reality, we should ask: What do You want to teach me in this moment? How can I emerge from this with a better understanding of who You are? Write down the things that have left you feeling disheartened and then rewrite your story.

Lord,

Use our pain to set fire to our passions. Your word says "I am fearfully and wonderfully made" (Psalm 139:4), so I will not bow down to the opinions of others. I will choose to believe that You mean what You say. I will take a "no" from the world and use it as an opportunity to "know" you more. Jeremiah 29:11 tells me, You know the plans You have for me, plans to prosper me and not to harm me, to give me hope and a future. I

Rejection

pray I will see that Your ways are better than mine. You love me the same as You love others. "For God does not show favoritism" (Romans 2:11). I will simply look at the rejection from others as redirection from You and rest in Your love.

Day Ten
Validation

———

*Those that are less seen
are no less important.*

———

1 Corinthians 12:12-27 (ESV)

"For just as the body is one and has many members, and all the members of the body, though many, are one body, so it is with Christ. For in one Spirit we were all baptized into one body—Jews or Greeks, slaves or free—and all were made to drink of one Spirit.

For the body does not consist of one member but of many. If the foot should say, "Because I am not a hand, I do not belong to the body," that would not make it any less a part of the body. And if the ear should say, "Because I am not an eye, I do not belong to the body," that would not make it any less a part of the body. If the whole body were an eye, where would be the sense of hearing? If the whole body were an ear, where would be the sense of smell? But as it is, God arranged the members in the body, each one of them, as he chose. If all were a single member, where would the body be? As it is, there are many parts, yet one body.

The eye cannot say to the hand, "I have no need of you," nor again the head to the feet, "I have no need of you." On the contrary, the parts of the body that seem to be weaker are indispensable, and on those parts of the body that we think less honorable we bestow the greater honor, and our unpresentable parts are treated with greater modesty, which our more presentable parts do not require. But God has so composed the body, giving greater honor to the part that lacked it, that there may be no division in the body, but that the members may have the same care for one another. If one member suffers, all suffer together; if one member is honored, all rejoice together. Now you are the body of Christ and individually members of it."

Today's reading is much longer. I wish this were required reading of every person who has said yes to Jesus. If I could sum up these 15 imperative verses into one statement, it would be this: *You matter.* The Lord could not have spelled it out more clearly that He created us to reflect Him in the most unique ways. That means God doesn't just give us permission, He commands us to look different, sound different, think different and function in different capacities.

There's something about a Jesus girl that doesn't measure her worth by her failures or success. A free girl that doesn't strive to be seen or crave affirmation- that's the kind of girl that is sure of her calling and rooted in her faith. She does her job and does it well because she loves the part she plays.

The body is designed to function where its parts work together. They aren't made for selfish motive, to seek recognition or to put more emphasis on one over the other. They are simply created to sustain life. Yet sometimes in the body of Christ, we lose the plot. Church can become more about what happens on Sundays than what happens in our hearts. It can become less about community and more about comparing. We start to realize that certain parts of the body appear more effective and seem more appealing. It's easy to notice the hands and feet of Christ. The head is seen by all and it wouldn't be supported if not for the neck. Yet, most of us become intimidated by what is seen and begin to feel less than. What do we do when we feel like an armpit, toenail or nose hair?

We attempt to become something we're not.

When we chase after the desire to feel important, we tend to focus on being seen, heard or even validated. Our confidence can be swayed by the ways others do or don't see us. Hope placed in man is a shattering waiting to happen. It's like playing baseball in a glass room; something is bound to be broken. When we allow ourselves to become defined by people, we will believe the definitions they give us. It's a breeding ground for discontentment and a disheartened spirit.

Let's revisit Nehemiah. You could describe him as a toenail in the body of Christ. His job when we meet him is a cup bearer to the king. He drank from the king's cup first to make sure it wasn't poisoned. What a job!

When he hears about the state of Jerusalem and the wall that once provided safety was in complete ruin, he sat down and cried. I love what he does next. He acts on the burden God gave him and asks permission from the king to leave his job and go rebuild the wall. That's crazy and took a great deal of courage. The king supported him and the people responded. Moment of triumph! However, when the enemies of the Jews heard Nehemiah's plans, they threatened him, taunted him and tried everything in their power to bring him down.

Validation

Nehemiah 4:8 (ESV)

"And they all plotted together to come and fight against Jerusalem and to cause confusion in it."

Nehemiah took their votes of no confidence and remained focused. When others tried to shut him down, he never stopped strategizing, building and working on the task the Lord assigned him. The only one who could sway his heart was the Lord because the only validation he needed, was knowing the Lord was with him.

Nehemiah 4:14 (ESV)

"(Nehemiah speaking) And I looked and arose and said to the nobles and to the officials and to the rest of the people, 'Do not be afraid of them. Remember the Lord, who is great and awesome, and fight for your brothers, your sons, your daughters, your wives, and your homes.'"

Words to live by right there! *Don't trust in their words. Don't even trust in yours, trust in His.* The danger in seeking acceptance from others is their praise with puff you up and their criticisms will cut you to the core. Today and every day I don't need approval, I need anointing. The more I find my worth in the word of God, the less I find it in the words of others.

Every part has a significant role in the body of Christ. Eyes to see, ears to hear, hands and feet to work. Internal organs aren't seen, but they keep us alive. We'd be in a world of trouble without them. And toenails, they're important too. They protect soft tissues, help toes provide stability and balance and they sure do polish up nice!

What's most important isn't what we contribute in this world, but allowing God to have the final say in our lives. It is to let Him see our hearts and whisper His love into us. There is nothing more precious than moments with Him. When I am vulnerable with God, I am validated by Him.

Lord,

We live in a loud world where everyone has a voice. Today I pray that Your voice would silence all the rest. Allow me to hear You above the crowd and become comfortable and confident in the things You say. I want to crave time in Your word because I meet You on the pages of scripture. Help me cast aside the need to please anyone other than You.

Day Eleven
Moving On

---

*If you stay stuck in what was,
you'll miss what is and
will never see what could be.*

Psalm 126:5 (ESV)
"Those who sow in tears shall reap with shouts of joy!"

I'm blessed to be the granddaughter of one of the most stubborn men I ever knew. Once he set his mind to do something, there was absolutely no stopping him. He was full of ideas and unafraid of hard work. His ways were his ways and he was stuck in them…until he saw a better way, then he'd chase it down. Do you know anyone like that? Are you cut from the same cloth?

There was one thing that remained a constant variable in his life that never changed: he lived for his family. He worked for us. Sweat for us. Bled for us and gave until it hurt. In his last few days, he held on way past his time. He was in pain beyond what his body could stand, but he held on because all of us hadn't made it in to hug his neck and say our goodbyes. I don't think he was afraid of dying, but the patriarch of our family was afraid of what we might do without him keeping us all in line.

He also knew his death would be the hardest thing some of us would ever have to walk through. Fifteen years later I still cry, as I type these words. I miss him so much.

When the suffering became more than my mom could endure, she propped herself up by his bedside, leaned over and spoke straight to his spirit. "It's okay to go home, Daddy. We'll be fine and we'll see you again. This isn't goodbye, so it's okay for you to go. You can let go." Within the next 24 hours he was with Jesus.

Doctors will tell you that when people are in the dying process but are holding on longer than needed, they just need permission to pass. They need someone to tell them they can let go, things will be fine. It's an incredibly hard thing to do, but what's necessary isn't generally what's easy.

How often do we hold onto something or someone longer than we should?
Someone hurts us and we replay it over and over.
We allow our past to hold us captive to our future.
We sit in the sadness of a season that God has changed.
We allow fear to pin us down.
A past failure blocks a future success.
An unhealthy relationship takes its toll on healthy ones.
A hesitation to a transition that we know must take place.

It's not the events in our lives that have power over us; it's the meaning we assign them. When plans backfire and don't turn out the way we thought they would, it can be difficult to see any good in the future. I have faced some grave disappointments, bitter betrayals and deep wounds from those I never expected. What made it so difficult to move past wasn't my doubt in people; it was my doubt in God. If He didn't protect me the first time, what makes me think He'll do it the second? Why should I charge into the future with a God-sized vision if I don't feel I have His God-sized protection? It can be more comfortable to stay in my misery than change my mentality. *Getting over* something and *moving on* are not the same thing. Like riding a bike, we have to keep moving forward if we want to make progress. When seasons change, it forces a response.

We know when it's time to leave something behind. Our heart leaves first. That happens on its own. The hard part is following its lead.

After every tear has been emptied and you're done living in the pain of the past, it's time to come out of the season you've been stuck in for too long. You may be mourning, but don't let that stop you from moving. We may never stop caring, hurting, or holding onto hope but we accept it's not ours to change.

Genesis 19:14-16 (ESV)
'So Lot went out and said to his sons-in-law, who were to marry his daughters, "Up! Get out of this place, for the Lord is about to destroy the city." But he seemed to his sons-in-law to be jesting.

As morning dawned, the angels urged Lot, saying, "Up! Take your wife and your two daughters who are here, lest you be swept away in the punishment of the city." But he lingered. So the men seized him and his wife and his two daughters by the hand, the Lord being merciful to him, and they brought him out and set him outside the city."

Bare Naked Truths

God destroyed the city.

Here are some take aways.

It was necessary for Lot to shrink his circle to only those who could see what God was doing. His sons-in-laws didn't go into his next season with him; those he thought would always be there. In fact, if you go back and reread it, God removed them. He surrounded Lot with the ones he needed.

God destroyed the city before the city destroyed Lot, but his lingering caused damage. Rather than defining that horrific event, he allowed it to define him. He stayed in an unhealthy place for so long that it affected him. The sin around him became the sin in him. Yes, he got out of Sodom and Gomorrah, but not all of Sodom & Gomorrah got out of him. He lost his wife and became a drunk who ended up fathering his grandchildren. I know, gross. Lingering can have dreadful consequences.

When we leave, we must leave the past behind. What's behind us isn't intended to go forward with us into our next season. The path is simply what leads you to your promise.

Your path is your path. People might not understand the things God has called you to. It's okay. Keep going and don't stop.

Today I pray you move on from that thing that has you stuck. If it's squeezing the life out of you, it's certainly not depositing life into you. Remember, Jesus came so that we could *"have life and have it to the full"* (John 10:10, NIV). By redirecting our thoughts back to Him, we give him the best of us in the worst of circumstances.

Move forward into the unknown. Here's your permission slip: You can let go. Things will be fine. He has the greatest adventures waiting for you. Say it with me: "I'm Ready!"

Lord,

Thank You for being the kind of God that doesn't allow me to stay where I'm at. You call me to face my fears and trust Your heart, even when it's the hardest thing to do. I believe You have something far better for me than what I leave behind. As long as I'm walking with You, I'm happy to go where You're taking me- even when I can't see.

Day Twelve
Hustle

———

God's plan works when we do.

———

Ecclesiastes 9:10 (NIV)

"Whatever your hand finds to do, do it with all your might"

God's will doesn't happen to us, it happens through us.

One of my favorite authors is Suzanne Eller. She has also written a few books that are all worth reading. She has an amazing gift of connecting scripture with storytelling and it hooks me every time.

In her Believing Big series on her blog, she tells this story:

"I worked in a grocery store from the time I was 15 all the way through my first year of college. I quickly learned the words, "Spill on aisle 2" could mean almost anything.

Pee was yuk (and not technically a spill). Sugar and flour were fairly easy to sweep. Jelly was no fun.

The worst was syrup.

Syrup was fluid, so it seeped into cracks and hidden escape routes. It was sticky so a mop or wet rag didn't work. A hot rag was required. Glass shards hid in its sticky fingers, so you were pretty much guaranteed to get cut. Even if you didn't, you worried that a sliver of glass was stuck somewhere on the floor, and the next spill on Aisle 2 would be someone's blood.

When I graduated to cashier, I was ecstatic. No more spills.

Until the day I was talking with a customer and missed the bag, dropping an extra-large glass bottle of Griffin's syrup. It shattered at my feet. There's nothing more exciting than having 32 ounces of syrup splattered in a 2' x 2' space with broken glass and syrup clinging to almost every available surface, including me."

Sometimes, we can fall into the trap of thinking that we only have to do the "grunt" work until God promotes us, only to find out, it's all grunt work. Suzie may have had to clean up the syrup, but I can guarantee you, she got her paycheck!

Players who win games show up to practice. People with fit bodies go to the gym. Following Jesus isn't a fix-all, it's quite the opposite. Our faith calls us into action and requires us to put our hands to the plow. We are promised hope and a future, plans to prosper in all that we do (Jeremiah 29:11).

Promise: a legally binding declaration that gives the person to whom it is made a right to expect or to claim the performance or forbearance of a specified act.

Prosper: flourish physically; grow strong and healthy. Make successful.

Although we tend to think of prosperity as something to be gained, it's actually something God gives us to give away. We are prosperous when we are healthy and strong in our relationship with Him. The Bible refers to it as being fruitful. It happens when the things that flow from us are intentional to show the love of Christ. When we allow Jesus to fill our hearts with love, joy, peace, patience, kindness, goodness, faithfulness, gentleness and self-control, we allow Him to prosper us. We have to make room for Him and that requires work.

Promises and prosperity, come from God, accomplishes His will, and changes the world.

Receiving the promise requires *nothing*. Obtaining it requires *much*.

Abraham was given quite a few promises in his lifetime and the common thread among all of them was the call to action that accompanied them. God spoke to Abraham:

"Go, walk through the length and breadth of the land, for I am giving it to you" Genesis 13:17 (NIV).

Touch it, see it, put it in your line of sight and then throw up blinders to everything else. Sometimes we have to keep the promise within reach. When the Lord gave this command to Abe, he'd gone too long without a reminder and he needed God to reel him back in. This was God's loving way of saying, "Hey Bud! Don't be lazy. Snap out of your complacency and actively move the ball forward." You've got your promise, so here's the plan: do something today that gets you one step closer to it.

Hustle

Promises require action: stand up for something, forgive someone, pursue a passion, or quit a job.

Go, walk (Genesis 13:17 NIV)
Rise up (Ezra 10:4 NIV)
Take heart (Matthew 9:22 NIV)

Sometimes, the action is to simply "be."

Be strong and courageous (Joshua 1:9 NIV)
Be fruitful and multiply (Genesis 35:11 NLT)
Be still and know (Psalm 46:10 ESV)

It takes action to get to it, go through it, and hold on to it. Let us not confuse *action* with *effort*. When God made Abraham a promise, it didn't just plop in his lap. He had to be obedient, allow God to work on him, experience a relationship with God, endure testing and trials, and the list goes on. It's funny how we all want the end results, but not necessarily the pain and hustle of getting there.

I have a few promises that God has given me and some of them I don't even like! Yup. I just said that. It's not what I would've picked. Sometimes I wonder why on earth I am pursuing something I never asked for. But, oh the journey! I wouldn't trade it for anything. The lessons have been rich. The love that surrounds what God calls me to is a force to be reckoned with. The purpose that has emerged from the pain of the pursuit has left me speechless (which is a very, very hard thing to do). The refining that was once uninvited has become precious to me.

I would dare to say that the Abraham, who was given a promise from God, was a changed man by the time he obtained the promise. He had to understand what it took to possess a promise from God. As a man who prospered materially and spiritually; he had to understand that the promises of God aren't *earned*, they are *given*.

Effort can't get us there. Effort can't keep us there. We can only receive through surrender.

Yes, Lord. I will walk this promise out, even if it requires me to love my enemies when they deserve my wrath. I'll choose to find joy in your sweet presence when I just want to be left alone. I will find you in my raging storms and know that no matter what, I can have peace. I'll accept that when I'm in a waiting period, I'm still with you and my heart can rest in that. I will be good and gentle to those who are harsh to me. And when I can't be kind, I'll just be quiet. I want to prosper, it's worth it to me. I know that if I can't learn to prosper, I'll never reach my promise.

It's not about what we produce, but what we reproduce. The more we give God, the more He gives us. And we somehow find ourselves in a place we never knew we wanted and we never want to leave.

So...GO, WALK toward your promise. Keep it within eyesight (you'll need the reminders that it's worth it). Just remember, what He gives you is just as beautiful as what He takes away.

Hustle

Psalm 1:3 (NLT)

"They are like trees planted along the riverbank, bearing fruit each season. Their leaves never wither, and they prosper in all they do."

Lord,

Make me a Psalm 1:3 girl. In a world of people that are withering and dying, I want to be full of life. Soften my heart and give me a strong work ethic so that I will be willing to do what it takes to fulfill Your promises in my life. I won't wait for people to come to me. With Your help, I will chase them down and live them out. I want to serve You with all my might. Thank You that You have a plan that far surpasses my greatest desires.

Day Thirteen
Forgiveness

———

Forgiveness can't change the events that have already happened, but it can change the events that will happen.

———

Matthew 6:14-16 (NIV)
 "For if you forgive men when they sin against you, your heavenly Father will also forgive you. But if you do not forgive men their sins, your Father will not forgive your sins."

Lord, he's not sorry, but I forgive him.

I remember saying that prayer at a stop light about someone I considered a dear friend to my husband and I. We let him into our hearts a little too quickly before examining his character. He seemed like a great guy and he was, but when our family went through a tough season, he turned his back on us and hurt us deeply. It took me quite some time to shake that kind of pain.

The weight of unforgiveness can anchor us in the wrong place. When we forgive, we take back areas of our heart that have been owned by someone else for too long. Anger, bitterness, a bend in our hearts towards revenge; it's no way to live.

God doesn't ask us to do easy things, he challenges us with the things that cost us. Isn't it true that the things we pay for have more of our attention? We are more likely to take care of things that cost us, things we've had to sacrifice for.

Choosing unforgiveness forfeits intimacy with God. We build walls around areas of our heart in attempt to keep the pain out. Unfortunately, it keeps God's love out and blocks relationships from going deeper. True love and unforgiveness cannot coexist. They're not neighbors, they're not friends. They cannot be residents in the same heart.

Anytime I feel anger or bitterness, it puts someone else in control of what my emotions are doing. The problem with that is two-fold, because God isn't in control of my emotions either.

It's a little too easy for us to feel like we are the only ones in the world that feel a certain way. Like no one else could possibly understand the painful events and hurts we've had to walk through. Not so. That's what makes following Jesus so incredibly amazing. There's no wound to our soul that He hasn't experienced Himself.

In His last hours, He ate a dinner with His nearest and dearest, the ones in His inner circle. These are the ones who were supposed to have His back. He shared with him the pain He was about to endure at the cross and that one of them would sell Him out, sheer and utter betrayal. They didn't understand Him. Some would say they didn't even attempt to relate to Him or maybe they couldn't. One of the ones Jesus invested in, prayed for, loved and cared for would sell Him out to side with men Judas believed could do more for him.

Are you nodding your head right now? Do you know the feeling? Do you have a name or two floating around in your thoughts? Yeah, me too.

Maybe the disciples didn't understand, maybe they didn't believe him, but they brushed him off like his feelings didn't matter. I wonder if it made him feel like *he* didn't matter? He told them, *"My soul is very sorrowful, even to death; remain here, and watch with me"* Matthew 26:38 (NIV).

It was the least they could do, right? *Just stay with me, I'm hurting, scared, overwhelmed. Please pray for me. He reached out.* They fell asleep.

What happens next hurts my heart. Judas enters with intention to abandon every memory, all the laughs and time spent together, all the lessons and the privilege of being let in to the inner courts of the heart of the son of God. He locks eyes with Jesus and Jesus said, *"My friend, go ahead and do what you have come for"* (Matthew 26:50 NLT). He knew why Judas was there; his lies would ultimately send Jesus to His death. Yet, He called Judas FRIEND…and He meant it.

Jesus had already made a decision to live with the sins of others and not hold it against them. Forgiveness isn't just a choice or matter of will, it's obedience to God.

He commands us to forgive in every circumstance:

Forgiveness

Colossians 3:13 *Bear with each other and forgive whatever grievances you may have against one another. Forgive as the Lord forgave you* (NIV).

Make allowance for each other's faults, and forgive anyone who offends you. Remember, the Lord forgave you, so you must forgive others (NLT).

We don't get to pick and choose which offenses are and are not forgivable.

I know. I don't even like reading those words and I wrote them.

It may not be fair; in fact it's probably not. They may not deserve it, but that's not what forgiveness is about. Forgiveness isn't our gift to our offender; it's our gift to God.

Why would he ask us to do such a thing? Lewis B. Smedes wrote in his book, *Forgive and Forget,* "When you release the wrongdoer from the wrong, you cut a malignant tumor out of your inner life. You set a prisoner free, but you discover that the real prisoner was yourself."

Jesus asks us to forgive. He doesn't ask us to deny the event or person who hurt us or bury it deep in our soul. He never commands us to release people from the respon-sibilities of their actions. Consequences are entirely biblical. There is no place in scripture that equates forgiving with forgetting. It's wise to remember, so that we don't become a doormat to the sins of others. We must remember to make solid future decisions.

Nothing about forgiveness justifies what was done to us. It's a decision to take the road less traveled; the same road Jesus took. Remember some of His last words He spoke as he hung on a cross were words of forgiveness, forgiving people who didn't deserve it. I believe He wasn't just talking about those who were killing Him when He said, *"Father forgive them..."* I'm pretty sure that reference was also encompassing us.

Forgiveness is more about trusting God with our future than our past. It's choosing to trust Him with the consequences of how that sin impacts me and my offender. They didn't just sin against me, they sinned against God. And although I want to step in so badly and control the circumstances, to do my best to ensure justice is served at the highest level, it's much more effective to get out of God's way and let Him have them. God is better at justice than we are. True justice takes a wrong heart and makes it right. When we hold resentment against someone, they hold a part of our freedom.

It's now God's place to bring justice, not ours. He can do it better than we can.

We might never see justice on earth, but we have to trust God with it.

Let's make a choice together: I will overcome what was done to me and not hold it against them. I will give them to God because He knows what they need. I will pray for them, knowing that it fills me with God's love and mercy. I will trust God to do in me what I can't do in my own strength.

Forgiveness

Lord,

Show me who I need to forgive. I don't want to live a life of resentment and offense. Your grace is too precious for me to not enjoy it in its fullness. Teach me to look past the person and see a heart that needs You. Forgive them. Extend Your love to them so they can be changed by You. I forgive.

Day Fourteen
Grit

High callings come with high price tags.

---

1 Corinthians 15:58 (ESV)

"Therefore, my beloved brothers, be steadfast, immovable, always abounding in the work of the Lord, knowing that in the Lord your labor is not in vain."

Have you ever heard the saying "No grit, no pearl?" I've always wondered what exactly that statement means. It turns out that pearls are a product of pressure. It begins with something small that causes an irritation — a piece of sand, grit, shell that which aggravates the tender flesh of the oyster. The oyster responds by building up layers of calcium carbonate around what started out as a foreign object that gradually grows into a pearl. You could say something beautiful comes from an unplanned intruder that "gets under your skin." A small pearl takes around 2-3 years to grow; a large one, closer to 10. The longer it endures harsh elements, the more valuable it becomes.

It would be so nice if we were called to play it safe for Jesus. I'd take much larger leaps of faith if I was certain they came without any hiccups or hesitations. This 'faith' life would be so much easier if everything fell into place. If that were the case, God wouldn't have instructed us to be *steadfast, immovable, always abounding in the work of the Lord.* He calls us to do what it takes to get the job done. That looks different for all of us, but one thing is sure: sharing the gospel is a high calling. One to which you've been assigned.

If you're not familiar with Angela Duckworth's ted talk on grit, it's worth a listen. Full of knowledge and research, she explains the common denominator among wildly successful people with one word: grit. She mentions what is referred to as the "ten year rule" in psychology, which states that it typically takes ten years of focused, persistent attention at something before it becomes successful. This reminds me of a word we just read about: steadfast.

She talks about people that stay in challenging environments and don't back down to their own weaknesses. The Bible has a name for that: immovable.

Then she explains that successful people are those with a specific interest and focus mixed with talent. In other words, they know why they are doing what they are doing and that's their drive. Talent can get you places, but it won't keep you there. In the kingdom of God, we call that, *abounding in the work of the Lord.*

Grit, by the world's standards, is doing what it takes to get the job done. In the eyes of Jesus, it's something developed in testing, waiting, irritations, opposition, and times when we draw near to God. Nothing we walk through is wasted. When Paul wrote a letter to the Corinthians, he had the idea of grit outlined to a T and the research hadn't even been done yet.

Why did he instruct us to be *"steadfast, immovable, always abounding in the work of the Lord?"* I think he understood that kingdom work isn't easy work. If we want to be successful, we'll have to have some grit.

Let's look closely at God's recipe for success:

Steadfast. A consistent person is a credible person. I lean on these types of people because they feel safe. There's something about the comfort we find in a solid person who remains constant throughout the years. In good times and bad they stay the course.

They are trusted to stay on task.

They don't change their minds constantly.

Their opinions are not easily swayed.

They don't rewrite the rules after every podcast they listen to or conference they attend.

They stick with it when there is no gain.

They may lose hope, but they never give up.

Out of all the Patriarchs in scripture, I wish we knew a little more about Isaac. What we do know is he was steadfast when he set his mind to something. When the land was in famine, he saw a need for his people and he responded.

Genesis 26:18 (NIV)

"Isaac reopened the wells that had been dug in the time of his father Abraham."

It seemed to be a huge controversy and people kept arguing over who the well belonged to. So, he dug another one.

Genesis 26:21 (NIV)

"Then they dug another well..."

And another one.

Genesis 26:22 (NIV)

"He moved on from there and dug another well..."

And another one.

Genesis 26:25 (NIV)

"There he pitched his tent, and there his servants dug a well."

After much opposition, he finally got to enjoy his hard work. Tenacity triumphed! That's what it means to be steadfast; one who can be counted on to get the job done because people are depending on them.

Immovable. We have an English Bullmastiff. He's obnoxiously huge and his name is Ace. We should have named him Boulder because he's as stubborn as one. He marches to the beat of his own drum and likes his beauty rest. When I wake him from his slumber, he absolutely refuses to move until he's ready. Will. Not. Move. He's not even afraid of my mom voice. Winston Churchill describes courage as a decision. It's how you know if you're called to do something or not. Are you willing to do what it takes even when it's hard? Are you willing to do it while afraid?

When David faced Goliath in 1 Samuel 17, he encountered paralyzing hostility and unbeatable odds. However, he didn't budge from his assignment. Rather than running from the problem, David ran to it with all he had. *I'm not backing down Goliath, the Lord is on my side.* He didn't pray the battle would be won, he took the Lord with him and went straight in. God called him to the frontline of battle, and he was a good steward. Then, God moved him to the next one.

Bare Naked Truths

Oh to be a David in a world of Saul's. The thing that set David apart: he didn't back down.

I can hear his thought bubble: *I'm going to Goliath or I'm going to regret it for the rest of my life.*

Not even Saul, the commander of the army, had the courage to take the risk David was. Grit pushes us to take the risks others are unwilling to take. Hardships do not give me permission to abandon ship. God's call doesn't change when the world around us gets ruffled.

Always abounding in the work of the Lord, knowing that in the Lord your labor is not in vain. The work may be arduous, intimidating and tiresome but it is not in vain. If we are on task, it is effective. God uses it...even when we can't see. We must fix our eyes on our *why*. Why are you doing what you're doing? Why do you need to cultivate relationships? Why do you tell people about Jesus? Why do you believe?

Jesus is my why. If I don't rise up with an overcoming spirit, I will be overcome. Let's look for every opportunity to offer hope in a world that is so desperate for it. That passion He's put inside of you; pursue it. Chase it down. Develop the talents that are natural to you.

Lord,

Thank You for requiring me to have a strong work ethic. Help me to appreciate Your sacrifice more and more each day. Take my selfish ambition and make it selfless. Speak to me in every circumstance- great and small and incline my ear to hear Your voice as I learn and grow.

Day Fifteen
Thought Patterns

―――――

Your thoughts can lead you into destruction or destiny.

―――――

Philippians 4:8 (ESV)

"Finally, brothers, whatever is true, whatever is honorable, whatever is just, whatever is pure, whatever is lovely, whatever is commendable, if there is any excellence, if there is anything worthy of praise, think about these things."

In this passage, the words think about translates into *make it your habit of thought.*

Paul, the writer of Philippians, is encouraging us to be intentional about our thoughts; to focus on what feeds our soul and starve what doesn't. In other words, we need to make Christ-centered thoughts our default mode. Sounds like a good place for a hashtag: #thinklikejesus. If we aren't careful enough to capture our thoughts, we will find they've captured us. Living a life of freedom is established through a focused mind.

When I allow myself to focus on what God's doing *around* me, I'll miss what He's doing *in* me. We can rest assured that the enemy will do anything he can to snatch our attention away from Jesus. He knows that if he has our attention, he's hit the

80

pause button on our destiny. There's a lot of power in knowing your enemy and you will always find him on the battlefield inside your head. Make no mistake, he wants your every thought and he has a plan to get them.

Several years ago, I took a self-defense class with quite a few ladies from church. It was a few weeks long and although serious in nature, we laughed our way through it. Mainly because of how uncomfortable it was. There's nothing like partnering with some of your closest friends and trying to take them down or scream in their face. Yeah, pretty awkward. We made some memories, but the thing I remember the most was the best form of defense: being aware. Attackers bank on catching their victims off guard. So we learned to *get loud, push back, kick them in the knee, and jab them in the nose.* It looked so easy as seasoned women would get out of strong death grips from these big men. It all boiled down to one thing: they had a plan before it even happened. They didn't need superwoman strength to avoid an attack, they needed a plan. Most attacks can be prevented if you know how to be aware in a parking lot, not walk by yourself, make eye contact, scream, and know where to give them an initial jab. Yes, we learned how to fight off an attack, but more than anything, we learned to *get in front of it* before it ever happens in the first place.

Here was my take away about our enemy:
We can paralyze his plan before it has power over us.

It's the thought that counts! Literally. The thoughts we entertain squeeze us closer to Jesus or squeeze Him out of us. Our focus determines our function. It's the thoughts that we give the most attention to that will organize our lives.

Thought Patterns

We live in a world of constant noise. Think about how many voices enter your head before you even get out of bed in the morning. Some of us lie in bed and browse social media, some wake up to music, our spouses or kids, and turn on the news as we eat cereal. Everyone has an opinion, many of them unsolicited. Media, blogs, books, knowledge, education- there is no shortage of information and ways to obtain it. Spiritual warfare is just this: God wants to speak truth to us and the enemy wants to speak lies. Which voice will we listen to?

When was the last time you identified where your thoughts were coming from? I caught a few of mine this week.

Are they talking about me?
I don't think I fit in.
Will this person ever stop disappointing me?
I don't do enough for Jesus.

What are some of yours? Go ahead! Write them down. Write them in this book. I know if you're Type A, that just stressed you out, but do it.

Solomon calls attention to the details of our thought pattern.

Song of Solomon 2:15 (NLT)
"Catch all the foxes, those little foxes, before they ruin the vineyard of love, for the grapevines are blossoming!"

Some thoughts may seem innocent and unintrusive, but with time, can bring utter destruction. Sneaky little lies creep in one at time and become familiar, accepted and patterned. The wrong voice can become a constant voice. We must be aware that the voice we believe dictates our destiny.

I know it's impossible to control every thought that enters my mind, but I can control what thoughts I entertain and where my thoughts dwell. I can choose to set my mind on what's in front of me or I can lock in with who's in front of me.

When God gave Joshua the task of taking the land God had promised them, part of that was to invade and capture Jericho, a highly fortified city. It was walled, well-guarded and built to keep enemies out. God spoke to Joshua and gave him clear instructions in Joshua 6 to march around the city six days and on the seventh day, the walls would fall. That meant six full days of feeling defeated, like what they were doing was a pointless waste of time. Six full days of questioning if they had heard correctly and questioning if God really had their back. They had plenty of time to wonder if this plan was really going to work. We can only imagine what it must have felt like to suit up for battle, get everyone in place and march around the city and absolutely nothing happen.

Wait a minute, I thought you made me a promise, Lord? I'm doing my part, now where are you? Have you all but forgotten me? What's on the other side of that wall? Triumph or terror?

This group of men had every reason to doubt, share frustration, and throw in the towel. I'm sure they felt abandoned and forgotten. Then Joshua steps in and makes a very strategic move:

Thought Patterns

Joshua 6:15-16 (ESV)

"On the seventh day, they got up at daybreak and marched around the city seven times in the same manner, except that on that day they circled the city seven times. The seventh time around, when the priests sounded the trumpet blast, Joshua commanded the army, 'Shout! For the Lord has given you the city!'"

I hope you caught what he did. It was brilliant! He reminded them of their promise and had them celebrate the victory before it happened. They parked their minds in the goodness of God. He had to remind them of God's words because he couldn't lead defeated minds into battle and win.

When I check my defeated mind at the door, He opens the windows of heaven. His words keep me focused on His purpose for me. What promise do you need to remember today? What perspective do you need to see? Whose opinion of you matters the most to you? What are you believing that isn't true and what are you not believing that is?

May we dwell on these thoughts:
God is gracious to me.
He is my protector.
He is for me.
I am His child
I am free
May His words dwell deeply in our hearts.

Jeremiah 23:29 (NIV)

"Is not my word like fire," declares the LORD, "and like a hammer that breaks a rock in pieces?"

Bare Naked Truths

Lord,

You know my thoughts and You know the battle that is constantly raging in my head. Would You bring Your peace and speak truth to me today? Truth that will stop me in my tracks and last. I want to treasure Your words and know You more intimately through them. Redirect everything that raced through my mind to submit to You. I choose to think on those things that are true, honorable, just, pure, lovely, commendable and excellent.

Day Sixteen
Hope

————

Bringing hope to a situation brings heaven to a situation.

————

Zechariah 9:12 (ESV)
"Return to your stronghold, O prisoners of hope; today I declare that I will restore to you double."

If I was going to be a prisoner of anything, I would prefer hope! I just love this scripture in all kinds of ways. It's written to the people of Jerusalem that King Nebuchadnezzar captured and brought to Babylon as captives. These Jewish exiles in Babylon were referred to as 'prisoners of hope' because God left them with the promise of being regathered. It was a reminder that even in the worst of times, their promise was stronger than their struggles. Their 'stronghold' was their safe place, the place where they met with Him, the place of His presence. Somehow, it doesn't matter if we are captives or free, at home or in a foreign land, we have the ability to find our safe place. God whispered in their ear: Come to me and I will remind you that everything ever taken from you, I will restore...*double*.

I never knew there was such a thing as false hope until having a front row seat to an organization that was unraveling slowly. Rather than getting to the root of the issues that were killing this place, the management would continually put its hope in anything or anyone who would look halfway promising or come with a pep talk based on emotion. It was a Band-Aid for a break and wishful thinking at best; a hopeful outlook with a refusal to embrace reality. Genuine hope doesn't turn a blind eye and pretend that all is well when in fact, it is not. Hope honestly evaluates the situation and says: *Jesus has a solution for this. This can be healed. This can be changed by His power. This can be used for my good.*

Hope stands in the face of real pain and invites Jesus in. It doesn't deny the pain, it gives Jesus access to it.

My youngest has a scar on her forehead she always asks me to cover. She doesn't like it and wishes it wasn't there. I always tell her, "Scars tell a story of something you lived to tell about."

She just rolls her eyes and says, "Oh, mom!" When she was three, she ran into the side of our bed and gashed her forehead open. I remember panicking on the inside while trying to keep it together on the outside. She, on the other hand, didn't seem too bothered by it. She even sat still for stitches after the doctor explained what he was doing and asked her to sit still. I'm fascinated by scars on others. I know there's a story behind them, something painful they lived to tell about and more than likely, wisdom gained.

We don't all have visible scars on our bodies, but we do have some on our soul. The deep kind that were once gaping wounds. You know the times you think you'll never get through and relationships that could never be repaired.

Hope

People fail us.
Finances fall apart.
Job's dissolve.
Our perfect plans don't pan out.

What we want and what God allows invites disappointment.

Hope takes my breakdown and makes it my breakthrough.

It is a choice to bring God's presence into every situation with the expectation that He will act in our best interest. Sometimes He changes the situation and on even better occasions, He changes us. Funny how that works...hope will bring us our greatest desires, but not in the most desirable ways.

We tend to give up when things don't happen in our timing or how we would've planned it. We can choose to keep going or shut down that part of our heart. We're always one decision away from taking a completely different path.

In Acts 27, Paul is on board a ship, being transported as a prisoner when the ship wrecks.

Acts 27:41-44 (NIV)
"But the ship struck a sandbar and ran aground. The bow stuck fast and would not move, and the stern was broken into pieces by the pounding of the surf. The soldiers planned to kill the prisoners to prevent any of them from swimming away and escaping. But the centurion wanted to spare Paul's life and kept them from carrying out their plan. He ordered those who could swim to jump overboard first and get to land. The rest were to

get there on planks or on other pieces of the ship. In this way everyone reached land safely."

Sometimes God will allow the ship to wreck so we will swim to Him. He might allow drastic measures to show us the difference between an anchor for our situation and an anchor for our soul. It's a good thing Paul's hope wasn't in the boat, the guards, or even the destination. Jesus is always the plan and with that comes a plan that has so much to offer. Paul may not have had the boat, but he still had joy, peace, strength, and protection.

We must be careful to place our confidence in Christ, not our circumstances. When Jesus is our source, we look forward to what he's going to do even if it's not what we want from him. He provides a way forward, sometimes a way out, and always a way to Him. If "a dream is a wish your heart makes," then hope is an ability we have in Jesus. It lights the dark and extinguishes fear. Wishful thinking is based on man's ability. Hope is based on Christ's ability. How will we know our own strengths if we never have to struggle against the odds?

Romans 5:2-5 (NIV)

"And we boast in the hope of the glory of God. Not only so, but we also glory in our sufferings, because we know that suffering produces perseverance; perseverance, character; and character, hope. And hope does not put us to shame, because God's love has been poured out into our hearts through the Holy Spirit, who has been given to us."

Hope

Hope does not put us to shame. That's such precious news. The opposite of shame is honor. God honors us when we hope in Him. There's a popular phrase that has been coined and has been hash tagged lately: *The best is yet to come.* We carry with us the ability to encounter His presence in every circumstance, good and bad. The more we draw near to him, the better we get. Keep dreaming big dreams and believing that God will honor them. As for me, I find hope when I find Jesus. It takes courage to invite Him into our situations and trust him with the outcome. Let's be brave together!

Lord,

If there is any part of me that doesn't have the hope you need me to have, I ask You to restore those areas. Give me God-sized dreams that honor You and take my life further than I could ever imagine. Give me a humble and contrite spirit that doesn't back down when life's storms come. With every test passed and trial endured, I believe the best is yet to come. When there's more of You in me, life is better.

Day Seventeen
Holiness

---

*Being holy is more about what we believe
and less about what we do.*

Louis Armstrong is one of my all-time favorite singers. I don't know that there's a better song on the planet than *What a Wonderful World* and he sings it so perfectly. Although he didn't write the song, he delivered the hope filled message to a very racially and politically charged climate. That was in 1967 and we are still fighting the same things now as we were back then.

Turn on the news any given day and you'll agree, it's getting nutty out there. Straight crazy. We live in a world of contention and chaos. It seems we are moving closer and closer to an 'anything goes' mentality and accountability is swiftly slipping through the cracks. Everything and everyone struggles with a great deal of confusion: people are confused about what gender to identify with, what religion to follow, what is right or wrong (if it even matters), and the list goes on and on.

What we used to call morals and values are eagerly being redefined and the waters are very murky. Christians are feeling attacked and non-Christians are feeling judged. There are so many different paths to take, it's probably easier to take none of them at all. But God didn't call us to a life of what makes us happy. He called us to a life of what makes us holy. How do we even begin to obtain such an intimidating idea?

There once was a young manager who was preparing to replace a retiring executive. The younger man approached the older, respected leader and asked, "Sir, I know of the legend that you have become as a leader in this company. Could you give me some advice as I try to fill your shoes?"

The older man pondered the question and responded: "Three words: Make good decisions!"

"That is good advice," the young man replied as he wrote this down. "And what is the key to making good decisions?"

"One word," the veteran executive replied. "Experience."

"And how do I get this," the eager young man asked as he scribbled "experience" on his paper.

"Two words," the retiring man answered. "Bad decisions."

God uses our broken and bruised past to set us up for sanctified living. What if the thing that we are calling *opposition* is actually an *opportunity*? We have a chance to carry his name in the day to day of life. What if holiness comes by way of us evaluating our part in a very confused and broken world? What if we are called to prayer before we're called to performance?

If we step back and evaluate all the "what ifs" that brought us Jesus girls to the world we find ourselves in today, I have to ask: Have we really been doing our part? What does Jesus require of us from this point forward?

Holiness.

When I think of that word, it's probably not what you think. I think of the lyrics Louis so boldly belted out:

The colors of the rainbow so pretty in the sky
Are also on the faces of people going by
I see friends shaking hands saying how do you do
But they're really saying I love you.

Noticing others, seeing value in them, extending kindness, compassion and care is so important. When I think of holiness, I think of common decency. Rather than an exhaustive list of restrictions of do's and don'ts, holiness begins in our hearts and is reflected in our actions. When our hearts begin to break for people, we are one step closer to it. You'll live it in endearing decisions. Being winsome. Inviting. The gospel isn't behavior focused, it's belief focused. Jesus believed in people and so should we. The more we spend time with him, the more our choices will reflect that.

1 Peter 1:16 (NIV)
He says: *"Be holy because I am holy."*

The word holy means sacred. I don't know about you, but that's not generally a word I associate myself with. I definitely haven't earned it and on good days, it's a stretch to say I've properly received it. However, Jesus calls us to stand out in sacredness because He says we already are. Holiness was made attainable through the cross.

Why is it so hard to believe that we are loved and pursued? Why can't we believe we are created perfectly by the perfect one and He has a perfect plan? Don't be distracted over church attendance, religious rules and random acts of service. That's not what Jesus came to offer. The root of conflict in our hearts is a rejection of truth. It's not the kind of truth that defines life-restricting rules. It's the kind that defines life-giving relationship. We have to believe our God and His word. We have to believe that we are who He says we are and that others are too. The decisions we make daily either invite holiness or drown it out. They display truth to the point of drawing people in. So, I've asked the Lord, *"Do I make holiness look good?"*

2 Chronicles 7:14 (NIV)

"If my people, who are called by my name, will humble themselves and pray and seek my face and turn from their wicked ways, then I will hear from heaven, and I will forgive their sin and will heal their land."

My people. The ones who claim Christ and follow him. He's not addressing the immoral or confused. He's addressing his own. The war is won through humility and prayer. The battle that is the most urgent to fight is the one on our knees. It's a battle for our hearts and the hearts of those who are all around us. Nehemiah not only prayed for those who turned their backs on God, he repented for them. He didn't see himself as above their sin or incapable of doing the same things and neither should we. He went to God and said, *"Lord forgive us."* Ultimately, we play a part in our current realities: news feeds, what's trending and the latest buzz. Let's not undermine our influence. Headlines should spark ministry, not madness. Sure, we can abstain from ungodly thoughts and actions, but first we should abstain from the things that pull us from spending time in scripture and prayer. Abstain from busyness and the things that fill the places in our hearts where grace and love is needed.

Abstain from the thought that the love of God isn't enough- it is.

Lord,

Thank You for being the perfect model of wholesome living. Show me how to carry Your name with integrity and honesty. Draw me closer to You and Your ways. Allow my life to reflect You in a way that brings honor to You. Will You open my eyes to see Your goodness and give me a desire to follow Your ways?

Day Eighteen
Patience

---

*I'm after the promise,
but I'm developed in the process.*

Hebrews 10:36 (NLT)

"Patient endurance is what you need now, so that you will continue to do God's will. Then you will receive all that he has promised."

You know what would be really amazing? If God sent a game plan attached to the promises He gives us. I don't know about you, but I'd really appreciate a timeline, directional signs, and an owner's manual for every single promise He sends my way. I'm the kind of girl that likes to know when, where, and how things will take place. Control Freak? Maybe. But us planners like to be in the know.

In Genesis 16 is the story of two fellow control freaks. Abram and Sarai were a much older couple. In today's society, they would totally be in the old folks home. However, despite their ages, they were promised by God, something big: a child. By all appearances, it was a promise that was a day late and a dollar short. They responded to God like most of us do when He calls us to God-sized assignments: they questioned it. *How is this going to happen? Why would you bless me, out of all people? Are you sure I can do this?* They dialogued with The Lord and decided to wait with hands open, ready to receive. They waited and waited and waited. With every passing year, the desire to have this child grew stronger. *Somewhere in the process of waiting, they became much more focused on the promise than the promise giver.*

Ugh. I know the feeling. We spend more time in our lives waiting than actually receiving. We wait for God to answer prayer, we wait on other people, we wait in traffic, we wait to receive healing, we wait for our kids to go to bed! Don't pretend like that doesn't excite you, Mama's! Here are some words we are all guilty of saying: *If I could just get through this. If I could only get from here to there.* And one I think you'll relate to: *I don't have time for this.* As a mom I've caught myself saying this more than once.

"You're taking too long to get ready. Hurry up! We don't have time for this."

"I need you to quit arguing, life is too short to spend bickering. We don't have time for that." (This one's true....right?)

"Please hurry, we're going to be late. We don't have time for you to...(fill in the blank)."

Yes, I've said them all. Then, one day as my youngest was tying her shoes and I was fussing about 'time,' I realized she was doing it wrong. So we stopped and I showed her how to tie her shoes the right way- the way I do! Don't judge. There's a right and wrong way for everything in my head. It got me thinking: how many lessons should we be learning while we wait? How many should we be teaching?

Please stop and ponder that for a moment.

Patience

I'm so guilty of setting my gaze on the goal and nothing else satisfies. Nothing else.

Sarai decided to send her husband into bed with her maidservant and surely they could have a child that way. Impatient much?

Genesis 16:4 (NIV)
"He slept with Hagar, and she conceived. When she knew she was pregnant, she began to despise her mistress."

D-r-a-m-a. Because of their actions toward her, Hagar was now carrying something she never asked for or intended. Of course Hagar began to despise her mistress! Isn't that the natural reaction to people who make you feel like dirt? God gives us very clear instructions on how to engage in relationships with one another: *"Love one another with brotherly affection. Outdo one another in showing honor"* Romans 12:10 (NLT).

"Be kind to one another, tenderhearted, forgiving one another, as God in Christ forgave you" Ephesians 4:32 (ESV).

"Let each of you look not only to his own interests, but also to the interests of others" Philippians 2:4 (ESV).

These words are meant to bless our relationships and cause them to thrive. The thing about relationships is they require us to interact in order for them to work. Anytime people interact with each other, there is always a risk of something not going right. Personalities clash, motives are unclear, communication is faulty, and things can get messy. Whew-wee, can things get messy? So when we willfully step outside of how we are instructed to treat each other, the relationship begins to spoil.

When we so much as put one toe outside of the guardrails set for us in scripture, we move from Godly relationships to godless ones.

When the Lord asks us to wait, we tend to start looking around and noticing all the ones that aren't waiting. The ones that are "getting it right." And we become filled with angst. Discontentment can do that. I'm speaking from experience here.

Abram and Sarai dehumanized Hagar. They called her, "slave" and often referred to her as "her or she." She became a vessel to be used as they tried to manipulate God's plan. The irony here is that all of this was done in hopes of fulfilling a God-given promise. God had made Abram and Sarai a promise, they grew restless waiting for Him to fulfill it, so they decided to lend God a helping hand. They stopped focusing on what God could do *through* them and began focusing on what God should do *for* them…and people became casualties.

I wish I could say I've never done this, but that wouldn't be true. I have to remind myself daily that when I take my eyes off of the Lord, I'm not the only one who pays a price. My choices have the potential to cause others frustration, discouragement, hurt, unforgiveness and so on. Either way, my decisions can cause someone to carry something they never intended to carry.

Hagar was hurt and she ran away. She wanted nothing to do with the ones who made her feel used and unimportant. Isn't that what most of us do in situations like that? Hey Hagar, I get you girl! I'm a runner too.

Patience

Genesis 16:8 (NIV)

"Hagar (He calls her by name), slave of Sarai, where have you come from, and where are you going?"

She wasn't seeking God in that moment, but He sought her. He sought her out to tell her, "I see you. I know you. I have a plan for you."

It's when we get in front of His plan that we're no longer running with Jesus. If we bypass the process and don't learn the lessons, He can't reward us with the promise. The goal is God-given and free of charge; the journey will cost us. We must choose how we handle the journey. I don't want to be a burden carrier, I want to be a blessing carrier.

We all end up carrying things we never asked for or intended. Frustrations. Hurts. Jealousy. Unforgiveness. Has someone else's actions planted something inside of you that you now have a responsibility to deal with? God sees you. He sees your heart and every time it breaks. He sees your tears. He sees your potential when others don't. He truly sees you. I'm grateful for a God who sees me. I want to be known for who I am, not by a position or a pronoun.

He has a promise for you and He has one for me. Embrace the wait. There is joy in the journey.

Lord,

Open my eyes to the details of my days. I know You are in all places at all times and desire to teach me Your ways. Teach me Your ways. Instruct me and help me to enjoy the wait of what You have for me. Help me to find significance in the process of obtaining the promise.

Day Nineteen
Unity

_____

We may not see eye to eye,
but we can see heart to heart.

_____

Galatians 6:2

"Carry each other's burdens, and in this way you will fulfill the law of Christ."

During World War I, in the winter of 1914, one of the most unpredicted events in history took place. On the battlefields of Flanders, the Germans had been in a fierce battle with the British and French. Both sides were dug in, safe in muddy, man-made trenches six to eight feet deep.

In order to honor the Christmas holiday, German troops began to put small Christmas trees, lit with candles, outside of their trenches. Then, they began to sing songs. Across the way, in "no man's land" between them, came songs from the British and French troops. Incredibly, many of the Germans, who had worked in England before the war, were able to speak good enough English to propose a "Christmas" truce.

The British and French troops, all along the miles of trenches, accepted. In a few places, allied troops fired at the Germans as they climbed out of their trenches. But the

Unity

Germans were persistent and Christmas would be celebrated even under the threat of impending death.

According to Stanley Weintraub, who wrote about this event in his book *Silent Night*, "signboards arose up and down the trenches in a variety of shapes. They were usually in English, or - from the Germans - in fractured English. Rightly, the Germans assumed that the other side could not read traditional gothic lettering, and that few English understood spoken German. 'YOU NO FIGHT, WE NO FIGHT' was the most frequently employed German message. Some British units improvised 'MERRY CHRISTMAS' banners and waited for a response. More placards on both sides popped up."

A spontaneous truce resulted. Soldiers left their trenches, meeting in the middle to shake hands. The first order of business was to bury the dead who had been previously unreachable because of the conflict. Then, they exchanged gifts. Chocolate cake, cognac, postcards, newspapers, tobacco. In a few places, along the trenches, soldiers exchanged rifles for soccer balls and began to play games.

It didn't last forever. In fact, some of the generals didn't like it at all and commanded their troops to resume shooting at each other. After all, they were in a war. Soldiers eventually did resume shooting at each other. But only after, a few days of wasting rounds of ammunition shooting in the sky.

You no fight. We no fight. What a reminder that we are all human, all children of God. What power unity can bring!

If we isolate Galatians 6:2 and read it as is, we miss the intent of the scripture. In order to read a scripture in context, we must read above and below it.

Galatians 6:1-4

"Brothers and sisters, if someone is caught in a sin, you who live by the Spirit should restore that person gently. But watch yourselves, or you also may be tempted. Carry each other's burdens, and in this way you will fulfill the law of Christ. If anyone thinks they are something when they are not, they deceive themselves. Each one should test their own actions. Then they can take pride in themselves alone, without comparing themselves to someone else"

I don't know one human being that is exempt from a burden. Chances are you are carrying one right now, either one of your own or one for someone else. I have friends that can smell burdens a mile away. They simply have to look at people and with absolutely no indicators, they say, "What's wrong?" It's as if God made them with a built in burden detector and they know with one look something is amiss.

Before scripture gives us permission to carry each other's burdens, it gives us the yellow caution tape- *watch yourselves, or you also may be tempted.* Then again in verse 3 and 4- don't let pride in. We are to listen to what others are going through without taking it personal. I like to say: don't get on the emotional roller coaster with others.

I was texting with a friend a while back and she was very upset. When I asked what was wrong, I hated what I heard. We can be so cruel to each other at times and a person she cared about had let her down, along with a group of other people. In an attempt to be a good friend, I asked questions. When I realized how angry she was, I reminded her that this person loved Jesus and was also imperfect and possibly acting out of hurt himself. Her response indicated that I should have picked up the phone and called her so she could hear my voice. You know those little dots that sit there for what can be an eternity? When the response came, it read: *Are you taking his side?* No, I wasn't in the least. In fact, I agreed that what happened was wrong and didn't want to minimize it, however, I didn't want this to allow the disease of division to infect a good friendship. I want to be a burden carrying friend, but I must first decide where I'm going with the burden.

It doesn't matter who the burden belongs to or where it came from, if we don't take it straight to the feet of Jesus, we will lay it across our own heart and build barriers that keep others out.

Caution tape: Some people aren't content to just allow you to be a sounding board. They won't be happy until you make it personal. Division happens the moment we decide to assign blame and demonize the people we are called to love; when we take on an *us vs them* mentality. I've done this more times than I care to admit. In fact, I know the yuckiness of what disunity can do. Every time I've ever cast blame on others, I'm simply marinating in madness. We must learn to *carry each other's burdens, without carrying blame.*

Quite frankly, when I'm offended, I'm as stubborn as a mule. I'm perfectly content to sit in my snotty attitude and invite people to join me, but that's not the kind of friend I need and it certainly isn't the kind of friend God has called me to be. I want to carry the hurts, offenses, pains, and worries of my friends to Jesus. Then, I want to get out of His way and let Him do His job. We need to soak in Jesus more than we need to soak in our emotions.

In Danny Silk's book, *Loving On Purpose,* he describes the statements we make about ourselves when we blame others. Blame is like saying:

I'm not ok and it's your fault.

I'm not doing well and you're responsible for it.

I'm powerless. I've given my power to another.

You're the one responsible for how I'm doing.

God tells us "*Come to me, all of you who are weary and carry heavy burdens, and I will give you rest*" Matthew 11:28 (NIV). When we carry burdens we can only go one of two directions: toward Him or away from Him.

The more Jesus taught about the kingdom of heaven, the more His disciples realized it wasn't as easy as they thought it would be. He was asking them to think extremely far outside of themselves and embrace principles of living they'd never considered. It was simply too hard for some of them and they left Him all together. When He remained with the twelve, He asked them, *"Are you also going to leave?"* (John 6:67 NIV)

It's not what we carry but where we're going.

Where are you going with the things that are weighing you down? Are we walking towards Jesus or away from him? Yes, we are called to carry burdens and walk through impossible challenges, but *if there isn't a hand off, there isn't a healing.*

We can carry hard things with confidence, knowing that when God is able to trust us with the burden, He can also trust us with the blessing.

Lord,

Thank you that none of the things that weigh me down are mine to carry. I know the most effective thing I can do with any burden is lay it down. Will you take all of these heavy feelings inside of me? I give you every uneasy fiber of my being and trust you with it. Flood my heart and mind and everything in my life that is overwhelming me right now. Speak to me in the middle of my mess and don't allow me to stew in my disappointments.

Day Twenty
Faith

Either your faith affects your feelings or your feelings affect your faith.

Proverbs 4:23 (NIV)
"Above all else, guard your heart, for everything you do flows from it."

I'm a bottom line kind of girl. Big picture, get to the point, end results... that's what I listen for in conversations. I remember when my husband called me because he found a dog he wanted. He went on and on about the breed, their temperament, why this dog would work for our family and every detail you could possibly need to know. Of course, I patiently waited to ask the only thing I was interested in knowing: "Is the dog free?"

That was really all I was interested in.

Maybe that's why Proverbs 4:23 has become my favorite scripture, it starts with the words *above all else*. Words like that should grab our attention in a hurry. The Bible is packed full of wisdom, encouragement and life changing truth. It is truth. So, when it highlights a main point, let's really look at what these words mean in regards to our faith. Guard your heart.

I can think of multiple things we are proactive in guarding: our homes, children, jobs, titles and positions, health, personal time, finances, opinions, but how do we guard our hearts without being guarded?

It's these sneaky little things called *feelings* that slip in and take control of our hearts and before we know it, our feelings are dictating our faith. *I don't want a faith that's fluctuated by my feelings, I want feelings that are determined by my faith.*

There's a new fitness place that is trending right now that asks you to wear a heart monitor while you work out with them. You strap it on just underneath your chest and there are screens that show your heart rate, calories burned and colors that will indicate if you are working too little, too hard or right where you should be. Just like any other thing, you don't want to be in the red.

Paying careful attention to our thoughts and actions is the best way for us to monitor our hearts. When we invite Jesus in, He repairs broken places. He instills love where we feel emptiness, brings peace to places that don't make sense and stabilizes the ground underneath us that has been shaken and stirred by the world. Yet, if we're not mindful to guard all He's done, the undoing can be swift.

You know the expression: *Follow your heart.* You've heard it, said it, abided by it. It's actually horrible advice unless our hearts are submitted to our faith. All too often, my feelings want to jump in there and go rogue. What we let in and take out is a direct reflection of our reactions and emotions. Just because something makes me mad doesn't mean I have to stew in bitterness until I become resentful and callous. If I don't lead my emotions, they will surely lead me.

Romans 10:17 (NLT)
"So faith comes from hearing, and hearing through the word of Christ."

We have to know how very important faith is in our walk with Jesus. We believe in an unseen world. Most of us have not seen God or angels. This is where faith comes into play. *We often trip ourselves up thinking that faith comes from us. I'm so thankful that's not the case!* The Bible clearly tells us Faith comes by hearing. When my faith is from God, it's magnetic. When it's from me, it's manipulated. When we try to "have more faith" or "just have faith," we're attempting to manufacture something we can't produce. Jesus loves us too much to ask us to do that on our own. He's fully engaged in building a solid foundation for our soul.

Faith is the opposite of us working to believe something...it's way easier then we make it. Hearing the voice of God is what produces faith in us. When we hear, we begin to believe. We were created to need Him. So when we don't engage Him, we feel distant.

The voice I'm not listening to has no influence over my life. The further I get from the voice of God, the more I fall apart.

In the moments when my emotions are at war with my faith, the question remains: Which voice am I listening to? Am I listening to the cackles of insecurity? Is shame dictating my day? Have I allowed guilt to pitch a tent in my attitude? Or is my frustration dominating my concentration?

It's noisy in my head but only the voices I give permission to speak have a microphone to my heart.

Picture with me a long grand hallway with polished wood floors and a red carpet running down the middle. There are beautiful chandeliers hanging from the ceiling, one every 12 feet and huge gold frames with portraits of men and women from the ancient of days looking wise beyond their years. There are name plaques under each picture: Abel, Enoch, Noah, Abraham, Sarah. Welcome to Hebrews 11, what is known as The Hebrews Hall of Faith.

Hebrews 11:1 (NIV) gives us the most Biblical definition of faith we can find.
"Now faith is confidence in what we hope for and assurance about what we do not see."

The rest of the chapter goes on to explain multiple people in the Bible that accomplished so much for God's kingdom *by faith*. It contains a recap of all the greats of the Bible that I sometimes wonder were superheroes because of their amazing victories. I want that! I love to win at things. Who doesn't? If you go back and carefully comb the Scriptures in this chapter, you will find they all have a very strong common denominator: they mastered the art of recognizing the voice of God and believing it. The first part of that is often easier than the second.

By the way, we got the dog my husband called me about. I'm a small dog person and although he was small when we got him, he's grown and grown and grown. I'm starting to wonder if he's actually a pony. I keep feeding him and he just keeps growing. It's funny how that happens- *what we feed, grows.* The more I feed my feelings of discontent, discouragement and doubt...they grow beyond my faith. I've learned my feelings can sabotage the influence of my faith. Emotions can't be trusted like God's word. I will not consult my attitude for the assurance that only the Lord can give me.

As much as we'd love to control what's going on around us, we can only control what's going on within us. The only heart I have a responsibility to guard is my own.

Lord,

Am I believing something that is affecting my faith? Are there voices in my life that I've given a microphone that I need to take away? Help me to hear Your words and receive them as truth in my life. Increase my faith to know you more. Drown out the voices that don't belong.

Day Twenty One
Grace

_____

Where there is no grace,
there is no firm grasp
on the work of the cross.

_____

Ephesians 4:7 (NIV)
"But to each one of us grace has been given as Christ apportioned it."

Grace. I wouldn't dare attempt to define it. It's far too vast and wide to contain in a single definition, so rather than confine it to a definition, we're better off describing it.

Undeserved, unmerited favor. Beauty for ashes. Access to the heart of the Father. An unrelentless pursuit of all that I am.

Grace finds me at my worst, gathers up my mess and assigns its meaning. When the catastrophe of sin has wrecked me completely and I am swimming in the consequences of my choices, He tackles my trespasses and allows me to grow from them rather than be enslaved by them. This undeserved favor can absolutely cover every area of my life: every thought, every decision, every hope, and every relationship…all of it.

Bare Naked Truths

Jennie Allen tells a story in *Christianity Today* that I all too often relate to.

"I almost died at summer camp when I was 11. We had all taken kayaks and canoes and miniature sailboats to a little island off the shore of the camp where we stayed for a few days in tents. I was eager to get back to the mainland. When it was time to load up, I grabbed three friends and we got a head start on our chosen watercraft, an itty-bitty plastic sailboat.

About halfway across, ominous dark clouds rolled in. Within minutes it was raining. I was in charge of the ropes that controlled our sail. The harder I pulled, the faster the boat went. Before I knew it, the metal pole securing the sail knocked me into the water. The ropes causing the sail to tighten and speed the boat along were now wrapped around my neck.

I vividly remember the darkness of the water as the boat dragged me. My weight pulled the already tight sail even tighter. I was the thing making the boat go fast. I was the tension. The boat was choking me.

I would pull the ropes away from my neck long enough to swim up and take a breath, but I could not get untangled and the boat could not stop. The power of the wind was so strong that I could only get a breath for a second, and then I would have to go back under the dark water and be dragged along. I wasn't strong enough to pull the ropes off.

Just before I blacked out, a counselor who saw what was happening kayaked over, jumped in, and untangled me."

Grace untangles us when we are about to sink. Just when we think we may very well go under, grace jumps in and pulls us out.

Grace

God initiates ways for us to thrive in Him. He came to us. *He* carries *us*. He gives us power to live right, talk right, feel right on the inside and respond to Him the way we were meant to. Grace isn't earned, jockeyed for, or bought. God's love is not based on performance, it's based on position. He loves us because we're His children.

I love my kids because they're mine. There's nothing they can do to make me unlove them. Now, there's several things they can do that will make me unlike their current mood or unleash my momma wrath on them, but nothing touches the love I have for them. I still claim them as my own; when they are well mannered or incredibly embarrassing, when they accomplish or fail, whether they grow up to be rich or poor, they are my gifts from heaven. I'm their momma!

There's nothing we can do to send our Father's love away. He has enough to go around...and around...and around. His grace, *when received*, makes us better. The moment we demand it, we undo what God has done.

Hebrews 12:15 (NLT)
  "Look after each other so that none of you fails to receive the grace of God. Watch out that no poisonous root of bitterness grows up to trouble you, corrupting many."

  Grace says: I have something I don't deserve. I'm thankful.
  Bitterness says: I deserve something I don't have. I'm entitled.

Pride will push grace away and say, "I've got this." It replaces receiving for competing, genuine care for superficial

114

gain, and humility for outright stubbornness. Pride is gross. It tells us what we deserve, when we deserve it, and convinces us our way is the only way.

John Piper wrote, "Be careful of giving up too soon, our emotions are not reliable guides."

So true. Grace is the best teacher if we'll be patient enough to listen.

Paul wrote Timothy a letter as a spiritual father to his spiritual son with some pretty serious spiritual truths outlining all he would need for ministry. It's the same exact thing the Lord provides for us to minister to the ones He brings us, including ourselves. Yes, I minister to the girl in the mirror all the time. Sometimes she needs a good pep talk! All that we need is found in one place: grace.

2 Timothy 2:1-7 (NIV)
"Timothy, my dear son, be <u>strong</u> through the grace that God gives you in Christ Jesus. You have heard me teach things that have been <u>confirmed</u> by many reliable witnesses. Now teach these truths to other trustworthy people who will be able to pass them on to others. <u>Endure</u> suffering along with me, as a good soldier of Christ Jesus. Soldiers don't get tied up in the affairs of civilian life, for then they cannot <u>please</u> the officer who enlisted them. And athletes cannot win the prize unless they follow the rules. And hardworking farmers should be the first to enjoy the fruit of their labor. Think about what I am saying. The Lord will help you <u>understand</u> all these things."

What exactly does grace offer us?

Grace

Grace gives *strength*. It meets our prayer lives, personalities, giftings, desires, sacrifices, challenges and makes them enough. It will take every wrong motive and use it for good. Grace will cheer us on to keep going when we feel like giving up and carries us further than we could ever go on our own.

Grace gives *confirmation*. We can count on it to speak to our hesitations when we feel unequipped. It shows up in feelings of confidence, peace and passion and will send people to speak to our insecurities at just the right time. It's the open door that takes us into our purpose day by day.

Grace gives *endurance*. During our weakest moments and times of suffering, God's grace is the only thing that pulls us through. It may not pull us out of the storm, but it will steady us in the middle of it. We need the reminders that we will emerge out of life's battles (and even bruises) better than we went into them.

Grace gives *approval*. Because of what Jesus has done and who He is, we do not lack significance. We can be encouraged by the approval of others (mentors, pastors, spiritual moms and dads), but we cannot become entangled by them. Nothing will slow us down quicker than looking for approval from the wrong source.

Grace gives *understanding*. It helps us. We can depend on grace when we need an explanation of the Scriptures. In our lowest and in our weakest, his words will be enough. There's no place His favor can't find us. It refuses to leave you the way it found you. It qualifies the unqualified, pays for the poor, educates the uneducated, carries the weak and brings peace to turmoil. Grace is the compassion of God poured out on us.

Lord,

Will You open my eyes to see Your grace in my life? I don't just want to receive it, I want to be a woman who extends it to others. Thank You for the undeserved favor You've given me, the times I know You've been there and the times You've stepped in, unannounced, and caught me when I didn't even know I was falling. Remind me of Your grace every time I'm tempted to step away from it. It's too good not to hold onto.

Day Twenty Two
Insecurity

Insecurities not faced by a Holy God, become reality.

James 1:5-8 (NLT)

"If you need wisdom, ask our generous God, and he will give it to you. He will not rebuke you for asking. But when you ask him, be sure that your faith is in God alone. Do not waver, for a person with divided loyalty is as unsettled as a wave of the sea that is blown and tossed by the wind. Such people should not expect to receive anything from the Lord. Their loyalty is divided between God and the world, and they are unstable in everything they do."

I was shopping with a friend one day at a bookstore when a book on insecurity caught my eye. I pulled it off the shelf and called her over. "Look at this!" I read her the title, subtitle and synopsis of the book and then suggested we get it. It looked like a must read, one of those books that draws you in because it sucker punches your gut with the exact struggles you're facing. She looked at the book and then at me and said, "I don't deal with insecurity," and started to walk off. I never miss an opportunity to tease friends or call them out when they've lost their mind. So I bantered back, "No, but clearly you deal with lying to yourself because we all deal with insecurity! I'm buying you the book, sister!" Isn't that the truth, though? I've never met a man or woman who isn't insecure about something in their life. I'm familiar with the feeling, I've learned to recognize the sound of its voice when it begins to speak to me. I've played with this demon far too much in my life. I know what it can do to you. There's a key word in James 1 that describes it: *unstable*. According to Miriam Webster's Dictionary, *unstable* means wavering in purpose or intent. I know you're familiar with that underlying fear that the ground underneath you is shaking. When I begin to feel unstable, I can rest assured insecurity has arrived into my situation.

The essence of insecurity is trying to hide from God. Think about that for just a moment.

Psalm 139:13 (ESV)
"For you formed my inward parts; you knitted me together in my mother's womb."

Can you picture that? The God of the universe, knitting? Creating people so delicately with such intent and love. We may not stop to envision a scene like this, but it couldn't be more true. Knitting involves a creator and the created. It's a handmade process by which the person making the knitted object takes great time, care, and detail into what they're doing. It's not something that is mass-produced, made in a factory, or swept together overnight. Items made by hand take time and hold a higher price tag. And whatever is being knit together whether it is a scarf, hat, a blanket or anything else has a very distinct purpose.

Insecurity

Insecurity rises up when we take our focus off fulfilling the purpose of God and strive to fill the purpose of somebody else. Sometimes life just looks more appealing on others. When we see something or someone we admire, it's easy to begin the "I can't" statements. *I can't do that. I can't lead at the same capacity he/she does. I can't contribute like they do.* And since I can't, then I won't. There's nothing like insecurity to back you down from what you were created to do.

A scarf, a hat and a pair of gloves all serve different purposes. They really aren't comparable because they are targeted to warm different areas. The same is true for us. We are all created to uniquely serve different purposes. Those *I can't*...thoughts should never even cross our mind. God doesn't call us to follow a formula, He calls us to follow our faith.

Have you ever seen the behind the scenes bloopers at the end of the movie or commercial? Those are my absolute favorites! I love all things real. When insecurity creeps in, it takes our blooper moments- failures and mistakes- and displays them on the screens of our heart. We're quick to compare the edited and cut version of others to our bloopers. The truth is, we all fumble our way to the end.

We can't have a custom made flare with a factory made branding. There are no labels in the economy of God. If He created my inward parts, why am I so concerned about outward appearances?

Insecurity says that what God put in us from the very beginning is not enough to sustain us until the end. It's a lie the enemy would love us to believe. What better way to deny the love, greatness and power, that He's placed within all of us. Rather than looking inside ourselves for confidence, we set our sights on the outside, yet God doesn't work from the outside in.

The infection of insecurity is contagious. When we're insecure, we have the ability to pull out insecurities in others. Those who don't feel like they are enough, will intentionally or unintentionally make others feel like they're not enough either.

Here are some behaviors that reveal a lack of confidence:
-the need to be right
-feeling threatened by the ideas of others and arguing why they won't work
-constant comparison
-not celebrating the accomplishments of others
-difficulty giving or receiving compliments
-struggle to be decisive
-chronic complaining and negativity
-isolation
-being overly available (people pleasing)
-lack of boundaries
-sarcastic or always funny (keep them laughing and they won't have to see the real me)
-always requesting reassurance

Where there is a soul full of insecurity there is a heart filled with pride. Although a confidence deficit can come across as humility, it's never humble to be so focused on ourselves that we aren't focused on God and others. The root of insecurity is pride and what an ugly monster that is.

Insecurity

It's okay to know that we aren't enough. We're not. But Jesus is enough and insecurity tends to forget that. The Jesus in us is enough. *Just because we're not perfect doesn't mean we're not purposed.* It takes great courage to be imperfect. We can boldly step into today knowing that there is no performance needed. Children of God have nothing to prove. Such great news! That's the kind of truth that brings stability. Let's set our minds on his truth and not back down.

Lord,

Thank You for being a solid rock. You desire to speak to us and we desire to hear what You say. There is security found in You that can't be manufactured anywhere else. Please don't allow me to be like a wave that is tossed back and forth. Redirect my focus from what is seen outwardly to what is experienced inwardly. When You have my heart, that's the best place for me to be. Help me to find security in You.

Day Twenty Three
Self-Control

———

Doing things on a whim won't take me as far as doing things in His will.

———

1 Corinthians 10:23 (NIV)

"'I have the right to do anything,' you say—but not everything is beneficial. 'I have the right to do anything'—but not everything is constructive."

A cookie. A new purse. A friend. We are wired to want things that make us happy, but not all of the things we want are good choices for us. Have you ever been intoxicated by the feeling of momentary satisfaction? Have you ever been swept away in rage over the actions of someone else? Our tendency is to react out of emotion rather than reason. It may make us feel better to feed our fleshly desires, but that doesn't do anything to feed the soul. This thing called self-control is sacrificial. It's intentional and it's a choice. We can get so caught up chasing what makes us happy, we forget to stay grounded in what makes us holy.

We all have an appetite for something. Some of us have an appetite for many things: food, fame, sex, money, power, attention- you name it. We watch as marriages are destroyed, wars break out, companies go under. All because a lack of one thing: self-control. The struggle is real.

Galatians 5:22-23 (NIV)

"But the fruit of the Spirit is love, joy, peace, forbearance, kindness, goodness, faithfulness, gentleness and self-control. Against such things there is no law."

Out of all the fruits of the spirit, this one may very well be the most difficult to master. We can cruise through the first eight with a smile on our face until we hit #9, self-control. The smile fades and a sigh breaks out. Self-control is the ability to walk away from something that appeals to our senses, in order to indulge in something that strengthens our soul. You know, it's really not as easy as it sounds…and it doesn't even sound easy. So what I'm trying to say is, it's hard. Way hard. The fruit of self-indulgence can be can tangible and satisfying, but the fruit of self-control must be trusted. Back to that fact that it's hard. It's hard to relinquish control and just trust. We are wired to troubleshoot our own issues because we know the results we are after. It's always been that way. The original sin in the heart of man had a selfish motive.

Genesis 3:2-3 (NLT)

"'Of course we may eat fruit from the trees in the garden,' the woman replied. 'It's only the fruit from the tree in the middle of the garden that we are not allowed to eat. God said, You must not eat it or even touch it; if you do, you will die.'"

Genesis 3:6 (NLT)

"The woman was convinced. She saw that the tree was beautiful and its fruit looked delicious, and she wanted the

wisdom it would give her. So she took some of the fruit and ate it."

From most of our perspectives, this is an *obedience* issue. God set a rule and they broke it. Naturally, we think God can't associate with them anymore and has to send Jesus to pay the price for their scandalous rule breaking. More than an *obedience* issue, there was an *appetite* issue. Eve couldn't say no to her own desires in order to say yes to God's. They ate from the Tree of Knowledge of good and evil because their appetite wanted what knowledge could offer them more than the life God had for them. *I don't want to do it your way, Lord. I want to do it mine.* Before every fall comes an appetite for self.

What made Adam and Eve so special was their spiritual discipline. Can you imagine a world lush and green with direct access to God? The Garden of Eden must have been one of the most beautiful places human eyes had ever seen. It was a place where they met with God. They were completely rooted in all things selfless. Then, they barked up the wrong tree, the one in the middle of the garden, the Tree of Knowledge of good and evil. One decision to feed their curiosity changed everything. In this case, knowledge was not power.

They cast aside truth and embraced their emotions. Yeah, we do it too. One moment of satisfaction for a spiritual death, a separation from God. Gratification throws a loop in sound judgement. Nothing fills the vacancy in our hearts the way Jesus does; no drug, no relationship, no title, or material thing. Sure, we can cram our soul with things that gratify, but it will never replace the only one who satisfies. We wake up every morning with a God who is in control of the entire universe: the spinning of the earth, the stars in the sky, every person, animal and good idea. Yet, still we often pick other things over Him. What gives?

He gives love and I often pick fear.
He gives hope and I melt into discouragement.
I exchange His truth for my doubt.
He offers new mercies and I walk in old habits.

I can't judge Eve, I get her. She got carried away by her curiosity and that's something we can all relate to. I want to be the kind of woman who makes choices that build my character, but sometimes my feelings can get the best of me.

Proverbs 25:28 (NLT)
"A person without self-control is like a city with broken-down walls."

Jesus encounters a woman like this in John, chapter 4, a woman who turned to men to fulfill her. Like a drug, her desire to feel loved was irresistible. Our greatest human need is to feel loved. It will start in our emotions, filter to our thoughts and before we know it, our actions have been altered. He knew the state of her heart better than she did. What did she have to lose?

More than she thought.

Jesus meets this nameless woman at a well and read her mail. He offers her rivers of living water from a well that would never run dry and she accepts.

John 4:16-18 (NLT)
" 'Go and get your husband,' Jesus told her.

'I don't have a husband,' the woman replied.

Jesus said, 'You're right! You don't have a husband— for you have had five husbands, and you aren't even married to the man you're living with now. You certainly spoke the truth!'"

Can I break this down in the New American *Southern* translation?

Bless your heart, darlin! Get a hold of yourself!

He immediately went to her root of self- sufficient indulgence and said, "Bring those things to me. If you are willing to set aside your desires, I will give you mine."

The very thing she was self- medicating with was bringing her further from her healing. We can make the decisions that feed the moment or we can make decisions that feed our soul. Jesus cuts to the chase. He asks for the things that trip us up, so He told the woman to go get her husband.

What would he ask of you?

Go get your resentment.
Go get your envy.
Go get your need to control.
Go get your social media outlets.
Go get your addiction....and bring it to me.

When we connect with God, He becomes our desire. There's nothing we need outside of Him and no space anything or anyone else can fill. May we desire His life giving power over our death bringing impulses.

Self-Control

Lord,

Help me when I'm tempted to stray from You. If I give You my emotions, I will trust You to give me Yours: love, joy and patience. Help me to make choices that build my character and make my soul healthy. Open my eyes to see the value of Your truth over my selfish thoughts. I want to have an appetite that brings You honor.

Day Twenty Four
Growth

———

There's nothing He'll let me go through that He doesn't intend me to grow through.

———

Romans 5:1-5 (NLT)

"Therefore, since we have been made right in God's sight by faith, we have peace with God because of what Jesus Christ our Lord has done for us. Because of our faith, Christ has brought us into this place of undeserved privilege where we now stand, and we confidently and joyfully look forward to sharing God's glory.

We can rejoice, too, when we run into problems and trials, for we know that they help us develop endurance. And endurance develops strength of character, and character strengthens our confident hope of salvation. And this hope will not lead to disappointment. For we know how dearly God loves us, because he has given us the Holy Spirit to fill our hearts with his love."

You know those people who have frequent flyer miles with the airline of frustration? That's totally me. I constantly have thoughts flying in and out of my brain wishing my circumstances were different. Just when I feel like I'm in a good season, with some pep in my step, someone comes along and jostles my joy. Can you relate? You're skipping along,

129

everything's fine and dandy and next thing you know, you've face planted on the ground and you've got some scrapes and bruises.

In 2015 our family friend, David, was diagnosed with small sickle cell throat cancer. The doctors found a 4 inch tumor on the back of his tongue and said the dreaded words "stage 4 cancer."

How does someone even begin to process those words? Three words can change a person's life. Being thrust into a diagnosis like that leaves more questions than answers and a level of uncertainty that takes nothing less than a divine intervention to calm. David and his wife reached out to a small group of trusted friends to pray. Then they reached out to more people and the prayer for his healing grew louder with more and more voices. Through the power of prayer, God brought people together that never would have unified. New relationships were born. The encouraging words of loved ones kept him unwavering. What started as the greatest opposition he had ever faced, became a beautiful opportunity for people to grow together.

He started chemo almost immediately and at his six month scan, there were zero cancer cells. There's three more life changing words: zero cancer cells.

Here's three more: God still heals.

We don't get to choose our circumstances, but how we respond to them- that's all on us. Not every season of my life has been God's decision for me. Sometimes I wind up in difficult places because of my own choices. Sometimes, the choices of others bring me to a place I would have never gone on my own. Other times, things just happen.

We can spend all our time trying to determine *why* and be incredibly counterproductive. I've spent countless hours attempting to decode my *why* before admitting it's beyond my expertise to diagnose that kind of thing.

Asking *why* has rarely brought me peace. It's never solved the problem or yielded the results I was hoping for. Tossing a *why* up to heaven has never helped me understand it more. *When I switch my why to a what, I move from spectator to student.*

What are you showing me right now?
What are you preparing me for?
What are you doing inside of me?
What lesson do I need to learn here?

Are you familiar with the story of Jesus calming the storm? He and His disciples were in a boat when an out-of-control storm broke out. Apparently it was so bad, it made these grown men (some of whom were seasoned fishermen), panic. They woke Jesus up to an all- out fear of death.

Matthew 8:26-27 (NIV)
"Then he got up and rebuked the winds and the waves, and it was completely calm. The men were amazed and asked, 'What kind of man is this? Even the winds and the waves obey him!'"

They could have easily thrown their hands up and questioned why something like that would even happen in the first place. I mean, he was sleeping on the job. But rather than asking *why*, they asked *what*. What kind of man does something like that?

Growth

In the middle of my chaos, I'm still a disciple. We are full time students in the kingdom of heaven, we are *not* full time spectators. Our past prepares us and our present serves a purpose. I'd much rather extract a life lesson from my experiences than bathe in bitterness. When I submit myself to the process of *what* God is doing in me, I grow.

History has a way of repeating itself until we learn from it. When everything inside of me screams: *Lord, change this situation-* and He can- I know the better prayer is simply: *Lord, change me through this...what needs to happen in my heart?*

Nelson Mendela had many teachers in his life, but the greatest of them was prison. He spent 27 years sitting behind bars, yet becoming more free every day. What some would call being *confined,* he described as being *cultivated.* Prison taught him to stay focused, controlled and disciplined. So our question today is: What is my situation teaching me?

God loves us too much to allow us to come out of things the same way we went into them. He strips away the unnecessary, unhealthy and unproductive to clear our vision to what is. When our answer is to run away, Jesus asks us to remain.

John 15:14 (NLT)
Remain in me, and I will remain in you. For a branch cannot produce fruit if it is severed from the vine, and you cannot be fruitful unless you remain in me.

Remain. Not just in anyone or anything, but remain in Him.

Bare Naked Truths

How do we remain?

Nothing grows without roots. Stay long enough for Him to teach the lesson. Give Him praise when you feel like giving Him a piece of your mind. Pray deeper. Love harder. Encourage others the way you so desperately need it.

Hey, if we're going through it, we might as well come out of it new and improved; stronger, wiser, and more equipped than we went into it. We don't get to decide what we go through, but we do get to decide how we come out of it.

The pruning of my problems is the proving of my character.

Lord,
In every situation, in every circumstance, I want to grow.
Rather than focusing on what's going on all around me, help me
be aware of what You want to do in me. Show me how to remain
well. If it brings You glory, I praise You in my pain.

Day Twenty Five
Gratitude

I can be grateful for what I have or resentful for what I don't have.

---

1 Thessalonians 5:16-18 (ESV)

"Rejoice always, pray without ceasing, give thanks in all circumstances; for this is the will of God in Christ Jesus for you."

There's a very specific marketing tactic that seems to work like a charm in today's society, the message that says, "You deserve it." Ad campaigns do far more than make us aware that their product is worthy of us, they've turned the tables and are now convincing us, we are worthy of it. Luxury car? You deserve it. Destination vacation? You deserve it. Overindulgence? You deserve it. It appeals to our inner most desire: self. In essence, marketing companies are selling entitlement. They are banking on our desire for gratification.

Research has shown that acts promoting gratefulness make people happier 100% of the time. This means what actually makes us happy aren't the things we deserve, but the things we are grateful for. Anytime we take our focus off what we want and place it on what God has given, we share the delight of God. The danger is when we start to notice what others have and we don't. It can breed feelings of jealousy, resentment and inadequacy. When those feelings are present, gratitude is not.

Matthew 8:28-34 (ESV)

"And when he came to the other side, to the country of the Gadarenes, two demon-possessed men met him, coming out of the tombs, so fierce that no one could pass that way. And behold, they cried out, "What have you to do with us, O Son of God? Have you come here to torment us before the time?" Now a herd of many pigs was feeding at some distance from them. And the demons begged him, saying, "If you cast us out, send us away into the herd of pigs." And he said to them, "Go." So they came out and went into the pigs, and behold, the whole herd rushed down the steep bank into the sea and drowned in the waters. The herdsmen fled, and going into the city they told everything, especially what had happened to the demon-possessed men. And behold, all the city came out to meet Jesus, and when they saw him, they begged him to leave their region."

Now here's something you don't see every day. Not just one, but two demon possessed men coming out to meet Jesus. They lived in the tombs because they were so violent, the town wanted to keep them out. That was the easy solution. But, Jesus doesn't do easy, He does real. He cast the demons out, sent a herd of pigs off the side of a mountain and upset the entire region. You know, sometimes healing is messy and in this case, it was outright gory.

However, something is gravely overlooked in this story- by us and by the people who begged Jesus to just go away: these two men were healed. And the town ran Jesus off.

Gratitude

Here's the thing: I've done that too. Maybe not the same way, but I've missed the miracle because I was irritated by the mess. Our preferences can blind us to God's provision.

How many times have we made an "I" statement that caused us to take our eyes off Jesus?
I want...
I need....
I struggle...
I prefer....
I don't like....

We can be consumed with gratification or constant in gratitude, but we cannot be both. Gifts, blessings, and miracles only bring satisfaction when we recognize them with gratitude. Happiness is found in grateful hearts; hearts that make the most of what they have.

"What separates privilege from entitlement is gratitude."

"I will practice gratitude to access joy." -Brené Brown

When we put on the glasses of entitlement, we become blinded to provision, opportunities, and God-given gifts. Oh how tainted our hearts can become when we focus on what we lack. If it costs us our contentment, it's too expensive. We run a great risk of opening the door to pride when we don't pause and give praise for what He's given...and what He's withheld. Genuine gratefulness acknowledges that God provides what we need and that's enough.

At the start of every new year most people make resolutions. We set goals, get ourselves pumped up and most of us fall off the bandwagon by February. This year, my friend Janelle made our small group "Gratitude Jars." It's an empty jar and it's up to us to write down our blessings and fill the jar throughout the year. I can't think of a better way to wring in the following year than by reminding ourselves of all God has done, lest we forget. Rather than setting a goal and focusing on a result, we are all working on redirecting our thoughts and focusing on our hearts. Grateful hearts have grateful habits. Gratitude should always lead us into action.

Being truly grateful requires me to recognize what God has done for me, verbalize it to Him and live like a woman who has been blessed.

As a mom, I love when my kids tell me *thank you*. It tells me they understand the blessing and aren't letting it go by unnoticed. In fact, the more *thank you's* I get, the more likely I am to continue to do more for them. What really grinds my gears is when they aren't grateful.

True story: One day I had noticed one of them had stopped saying, "please" and "thank you." When I sat her breakfast in front of her I said, "You're welcome," in an incredibly dramatic way, calling attention to her lack of gratefulness. She looked at me and said, "Mom, you know my heart."
Goodness.

Actually, I don't. *If we are grateful, saying it solidifies it.*

Gratitude

Luke 6:45 (NIV)
"For the mouth speaks what the heart is full of."

Where there is no praise, there is no power. Some of us have a long list of blessings that used to be our prayer requests and we haven't even stopped to say thank you. *Lord, forgive us.*

Going back to the people in the region that asked Jesus to leave, what kind of blessings do you think they missed? Surely, He was just getting started in that town. He didn't leave on His own accord, so that tells me He intended to stay a bit. I'm sure the chaos of demon possessed men and dead pigs all over the place created an inconvenience and uncertainty they'd rather not be bothered with. It just goes to show: Some see the mess, others see the miracle.

There are two mentalities: "it's all about me" or "it's all about Him."

Plan of Gratitude:
Write down the top 5 things you're grateful for today
Say it out loud! In a prayer, through praise, or even a testimony.
As you've been blessed, bless someone else.

Lord,
Thank You for more blessings than I know what to do with. Develop in me a grateful heart that doesn't ever miss an opportunity to give You praise. Will you guard my mind from entertaining any entitled thoughts. I don't want to focus on what I don't have, I want to find joy in what I do have. Give me eyes to see your blessings in every circumstance.

Day Twenty Six
Humility

When God changes our hearts,
we change the world.

Galatians 5:34 (ESV)
"And those who belong to Christ Jesus have crucified the flesh with its passions and desires."

I recently sat down and took a few minutes to journal the top characteristics of women or mentors I admire. I was on a quest to determine what it was I liked about them and what I'm drawn to. What draws me to certain people and what turns me off? The results were humorous because most of them shared eerily similar characteristics, but the one thing that was the common denominator on every one was *humility*. And here's the sad part: I knew I didn't have it.

My heart sank. And I asked the Lord, "Will you teach me to be humble?"

Have you ever prayed for humility? Oh, it's not easy. I mean, it's easy to pray for it, but becoming humble in a prideful world is like a fish swimming up- stream. You have to want it. You have to fight for it. You have to allow God to change you.

Humility

I began to pray for humility daily, asking the Lord to change my constant need to accomplish, achieve, and be recognized for my hard work. I seemed to miss the memo that the whole "savior" job was already taken, because I felt I could change people. The more I prayed, the more I started seeing my own pride. It was gross. Like, ewww, go away pride!

There was one event in particular where I was part of an outreach to bless children. It was an amazing outreach that anyone would be excited to be a part of. On this particular day, we were serving these children and in the process, social media was being blown up as all of us were posting about it in our excitement: tag, hashtag, check-in, likes, and oh, selfies. There we were, taking selfies, forgetting the kids. I stepped outside as my head began to spin.

What are we doing?
Where is our focus?
Why does this bother me? It never has before.
I left.

I got in my car and drove away, on the verge of tears. I felt like someone had died and was sad for HOURS. When I couldn't shake the sadness, I called my husband and explained what happened and asked, "What's wrong with me?

He quickly reminded me of the prayer I had been praying and said, "You're mourning because a part of you is dying- your flesh."

What might have been a silly selfie for some was a "look at how good I am" for me. And God was killing that desire. Crucifying it.

Side note: I'm not condemning selfies. Take them. Post them. If you're a selfie sister, I love it! And I love you. This was about my desire to be seen trumping my desire to serve.

Just needed to make sure you knew that. Now, carry on.

Deuteronomy 8:2 (ESV)
"And you shall remember the whole way that the Lord your God has led you these forty years in the wilderness, that he might humble you, testing you to know what was in your heart, whether you would keep his commandments or not."

This was a reminder to the Israelites to always keep in front of them that they couldn't and shouldn't do it themselves. *Nothing worth talking about, talks about itself.*

He will test us, not because He doesn't already know what's in our hearts, but because we don't. Every test is an opportunity to learn more about His nature and be changed by it. God gives us tests so He can give us trust. We are entrusted to carry His name, not make one for ourselves. The less humble we are, the less likely we are to keep His commandments.

Proverbs 11:2 (NLT)
"Pride leads to disgrace, but humility comes wisdom."

The minute we think we can do it on our own, God will allow us to do just that and disgrace is sure to follow. I'd rather have His grace than my disgrace. When I choose humility, I choose wisdom- every time.

When Peter and John were sent out to serve people in ministry, they walked into a city and a lame man was there, begging for money.

Acts 4:5-6 (NIV)

"Peter looked straight at him, as did John. Then Peter said, "Look at us!" So the man gave them his attention, expecting to get something from them. Then Peter said, "Silver or gold I do not have, but what I do have I give you. In the name of Jesus Christ of Nazareth, walk."

Two things happened here:

Peter looked at him, not past him. He saw this man as worth his time. I picture this scene with Peter bending down to get on his level and saying in the most sincere and excited way, "Look at us!" When we look people in the eye, we give them our attention and communicate the message that they are important, just as important as we are.

The message he sent was clear. It's the same message we should all carry: *It's not about what I can offer you, it's about what Jesus can offer you.* There was no selfish motive or intent. He didn't try to take credit for a good deed, he didn't even try to have all the answers. He simply offered the man God's love.

I want that attitude. I want to do more than notice people, I want to see them the way God does and admit when I'm not enough, I'm okay with that. Only He is enough.

The word humble originated from the meaning *near the ground.* The more we lower ourselves, the more humble we become. Charles Spurgeon said, "Every Christian has the choice of being humble or being humbled." It's the difference between bowing down and falling down.

The lower we bow down, the higher we will rise.

Here are some characteristics of humility. How I desire to have all of these! One day in heaven, I will. Until then, they are simply guidelines and prayer targets:

Outward focus. Rather than walking into a room with a "here I am" mentality, people with outward focus constantly seek others out and engage in their lives. They ask questions, take interest and connect. They don't show up to be seen, they show up to care.

Believes in others. Remember the eye contact? When we believe in others, we acknowledge the ability of God to use all of us for His good and it eliminates the need to compete.

Loves to learn and doesn't mind asking for help. They who understand that there are other ways of doing things, and those ways work. Things don't always have to be done their way for it to be "right."

Forgives. Humble people recognize their own mistakes and sins and don't hold the sins of others against them. They understand we live in an imperfect world, full of sin and the only way to make it out alive is to forgive.

Knows how to hush. Keeping it shut is a skill not all have learned. If that's you, you're not alone. Me too sister, me too. The person who knows how to hush doesn't always have to have an opinion or be right. They speak when it matters and keep quiet when it doesn't.

Welcomes honest feedback. They realize that honesty is the best medicine. *You can't fix what you won't address.* Humility wants to improve and get better. It feels comfortable asking for ideas, is open to what others have to say, admits their own weaknesses, and learns from their failures.

Celebrates others and shares credit. They treat people with respect and are grateful for the people God has placed in their lives. They have come to realize, we are all on the same team. When others do well, we all do well.

Lord,

Only by Your grace am I humbled. Today and every day, will You show me how to be humble? Will You decrease my appetite for self and give me a burden for people? Remind me in my daily routines to look into people's souls and offer them You, and not me. Increase my capacity to love.

Day Twenty Seven
Doubt

---

*Our doubts can define us
or defeat us.*

Proverbs 3:5 (ESV)
   *"Trust in the Lord with all your heart, and do not lean on
your own understanding."*

That feeling you get the night before a surgery.
The drive to a doctor's appointment where you have more
questions than answers.
The bills you can't pay.
The job interview you really want to nail.
Sending your kids off to school.
Moving to a new city.

How do we march boldly into life without hesitation?

There's something I can almost guarantee you...if God
asks you to do something for Him or begins to move you in a
certain direction you will almost instantly meet this thing called
doubt. I know this little booger very well and although he isn't
nice or fun to be with, his presence has developed me. I've
learned that if God can trust me to navigate around doubt,
disappointment, and discouragement, He can trust me to navig-

gate the dream He's given me. Every dream comes with opposition, even from the beginning of time.

Genesis 3:1 (NIV)

"Now the serpent was more crafty than any of the wild animals the Lord God had made. He said to the woman, 'Did God really say that you must not eat from any tree in the garden?'"

God created man and woman and gave them a purpose. Of course, with purpose, comes instruction. In this case, God told Adam and Eve not to eat from the Tree of Knowledge of good and evil. In other words, don't get caught up relying on yourself. When we root ourselves in that tree, the fruit is deadly.

Watch what happens next: Satan comes along and says, "Did God really say that?"

Doubt.

Leave it to the devil to not just ask any question, but the kind of questions that detours us from our destiny. *Maybe you heard wrong. Are you sure that was God?*

The devil is a master at questions. He's great at asking them and he's even better at getting us to create our own. It's the first interaction we see him have with humanity and it's on the heels of a directive from the Lord. That's the pattern we can be sure of: *When the Lord gives direction, the enemy comes in with a question.*

Did God really say…?

Anytime we entertain the enemy's questions, we sit down to tea with doubt. It's like engaging a terrorist; if you give them time and intel, they will destroy you. There's an old saying: *If you can catch the terrorist, you can get a hold of the mission.*

Satan will always question what God is certain of. It's his mission strategy to greet us with open ended questions and let us fill in the blanks. He knows if he starts it, we will finish it. We must not forfeit the end goal by making excuses.

After Jesus had fulfilled His purpose on earth and was raised from the dead, He came back to show His disciples He was alive.

John 20:24-25 (NIV)
"Now Thomas (also known as Didymus), one of the Twelve, was not with the disciples when Jesus came. So the other disciples told him, 'We have seen the Lord!'
But he said to them, 'Unless I see the nail marks in his hands and put my finger where the nails were, and put my hand into his side, I will not believe.'"

I'll believe it when I see it.

Sometimes our situations speak louder to us than God's promises. As crazy as this sounds (and I know it sounds out there), I think Thomas had the right idea. He didn't take anyone else's word, he wanted to hear it from Jesus.

Doubt

I'm like that too. I won't settle for second hand information when I have access to the source Himself. It was easy for Thomas to believe when he was with Jesus, but difficult when he was gone. So He invited Jesus into his circumstance.

This wasn't the place where he lost his faith, it was the place where he gained it.

When I invite God into my doubts and inefficiencies, He comes with His peace.

Recently, in the dead of the night, our alarm went off and we heard the door to the garage open. Can you imagine how fast we shot up? Our blood pressure skyrocketed and we ran to the door and silenced the alarm, not even fully aware of what was going on. I slammed the garage door shut, heart racing and in my panic asked my husband, "What do we do?"

He very firmly said, "We check the garage and then we check the house."

You know what I thought? *But what if we find someone? That's scary! Oh! My-Lanta!*

In reality, it would have been even scarier if we didn't check and didn't find someone who could have possibly been there. We would rather catch them outside of the house before they gained access. I was certain it was just the wind and we had left the door unlocked and I was content to go back to bed, but my husband flipped on every light. We went from room to room until every square inch had been checked. You can bank on the fact that in that moment, I invited Jesus in! *Lord, scare away the bad guys! Fix it, Jesus!*

Anytime an alarm goes off, we must do a thorough check. Is there anything that is a threat to my purpose lurking in a hiding spot I haven't seen yet? Doubts should alarm us to invite Jesus in. When we see Him, He redirects us from our problems to our promises. *If we don't deal with our doubts, they will surely grow and multiply.*

A seed of doubt planted in our garden of faith will blossom- it will bring fear where God has planted courage, anger instead of love, insecurity rather than confidence. Enemies of destiny are terrorists to our soul.

Jesus tells Thomas, "*I'm here. Stop doubting and believe.*"

It's that simple. Just believe. We can trust His words and find peace in His presence. When He shows up, doubt must leave. The only thing doubt has ever done for me was push me back when I should be taking steps forward. Today I will take a step into the right direction.

Lord,
  When my doubts come crashing in, remind me to invite You in. I don't want a purpose that has a question mark attached to it. Give me strength and confidence in Your promises. Thank you for your words that give direction and bring peace.

Day Twenty Eight
Rest

We must remember to stop before we start.

"Walk with me for a few minutes; we have something to talk about."

I live one of those lives where I bounce from place to place doing one thing after the next. Can you relate? Kind of like the Energizer Bunny on lithium batteries. I recently found myself squeezing in important conversations in between important events, on the go. No eye contact, no time to process, no intimacy. I found myself surrounded by friends, but connecting with no one. In an effort to accomplish things for God, I was slipping away from what my soul needs most: time. Isn't that what we all need?

To sit down and hush.
Calm our spirit.
Simmer our soul.
Turn our mind off and our heart on.
Time to REST.

In Genesis 18, Abraham is encountered by three men, the Lord and two angels. When he sees them coming from a distance, he puts in his lithium batteries and springs into action. Immediately he starts multitasking. He gets up and bows to meet them, swiftly gets them water to wash their feet, begins delegating and finds various servants to: make bread, prepare a calf, get them some milk, prepares a place for them to eat, and is on standby while they eat (literally: he stood by them while they sat and ate).

Does this sound familiar at all? Abraham is a pretty relatable guy. He's working diligently, doing all the 'right' things to show the love of God, honoring God with His actions. Have you ever been so busy doing things *for* God that you forfeit time *with* Him? Do you always feel like you should be on standby in case He needs you for something, so rather than dining with Him, you stand and wait for your next assignment?

I can tell you from experience, there's too much at stake to do that. We have too much time, too many lessons to learn, and too much precious influence that is gambled when we put our focus on the things we do.

Immediately following this encounter, the men get up and the Lord has Abraham take a walk with Him. I can just hear the voice of God talking to His boy, "Come on, son. Let's go sit a spell." That's a really nice way of telling someone to chill out and relax! Some of my most precious childhood memories are those back porch conversations with Pawpaw in the rocking chair watching the hummingbirds. Our talks were a time to connect before we set out to start our day.

Abraham and The Lord sit and converse about what's going on in a nearby city. As they begin having a heart to heart conversation, *Abraham ceases his striving, serving and working as unto the Lord to just sit and talk to God.* He walks away from all of his accomplishments and stops trying to achieve anything other than time spent with the Father. In this dialogue (Genesis 18: 20-33, NIV), Abraham pleads for the righteous people living amongst the unrighteous. He converses with the Lord and asks Him, *"What if there are fifty righteous people in the city? Will you really sweep it away and not spare the place for the sake of the fifty righteous people in it? Far be it from you to do such a thing- to kill the righteous with the wicked, eating the righteous and the wicked alike. Far be it from you! Will not the judge of all the earth do right?"*

Those are some bold questions to ask God. The more these two speak, the more they get to know each other and the more they begin to trust each other. Abraham needed to know a little more about the character and nature of God in order to lead others into His presence and God needed to know that Abraham's heart was in the right place. I want that kind of relationship with the Lord.

You know those lithium batteries I mentioned earlier? They are on the market as the most powerful and long lasting battery our dollars can buy. There's just one problem: They are disposable. They do their job in a mighty way and then die. Game over! It was a good ride. I personally have an affection for rechargeable batteries. They serve their purpose and when they have been pushed to the limits, they nestle into a port that is directly connected to the source of power which fills them up again. They are steady and long-lasting.

I recently volunteered with Convoy of Hope in disaster relief efforts. We were tearing out sheetrock, removing baseboards and nails from homes that had been flooded in our area. There's something therapeutic about smashing a wall with a hammer! It was hard work, but very rewarding. Right when I felt I had it down to a science, our Convoy team leader came in and yelled at us. "Everyone take a break. It's rest time." I didn't really feel like I needed one, but it wasn't a suggestion, it was a directive. So I walked outside with everyone and sat under a tree. They passed out water and did something invaluable: initiated precious conversation. Not only were our bodies becoming refreshed, our souls were too. We were getting to know each other better and connecting, which made it easier to work alongside of one another. It established unity and somehow gave us tenacity to get the job done. We had to stop before we started.

I don't know if this is what you think of when you hear the word "rest," but true rest is time spent with God. True rest asks God questions and quietly waits for Him to answer. True rest is positioned at the feet of Jesus in an effort to know and experience Him more. If we can get to know Him in deeper and more intimate ways, then we can lead others...but what we can't do is give what we don't have. Let's nestle into our power source today and allow Him to fill us. If we want to accomplish great things in life, we must first find great places in life to rest.

Lord,
I want to sit with You and ask You bold questions like Abraham. I want to know more about You and allow You to know more about me. Forgive me for making you an "on the go" God. It's not my accomplishments You are after, it's my heart. Help me not to run ahead of You or lag behind You. Position me to walk alongside of You in this adventure of life.

Day Twenty Nine
Struggles

_____

The more intense the struggle,
the more magnificent the strength.

_____

Genesis 32:28 (NIV)
   "Then the man said, 'Your name will no longer be Jacob,
but Israel, because you have struggled with God and with
humans and have overcome.'"

Like butterflies breaking through their cocoons, birds
breaking through their eggs or a seed that has sprouted and is
breaking through the ground, beautiful things emerge from
struggle. We can't expect to be brave if we don't have to face
fears, to love if we don't have to work through some hate or
gain wisdom without learning to work through some difficulty.

Every-true-strength is gained through struggle.

What do you think of when you hear the word *struggle*?
What situation are you facing today that you would define as a
struggle in your life?

Struggle is defined: to make strenuous or violent efforts

in the face of difficulties or opposition.

Struggling....to pay bills.

to like someone (or even pretend you like them).

to get past the shame of an abortion.

to overcome an addiction.

to get through depression and anxiety.

We all have different struggles but one thing is the same-we all have them.

Perhaps the reason I love the Bible so much is because the people in it were as messy as I am. They did not have it easy, in fact many of the men and women had major hurdles to clear while living out their purpose.

Of course when we hear the word "struggle," we think of Jacob. So cliché, right? The man who wrestled with God. More than just that moment, his whole life was an uphill battle. Before Jacob was born, the Lord told his mom that Jacob would be *stronger* than his twin brother.

Strength is defined: the quality or state of being strong: capacity for exertion or endurance.

Jacob was born in a power struggle, literally. He came out of his mother's womb grabbing the heel of his brother, Esau. He deceived his brother, stole his birthright and ran from home. Follow Jacob throughout multiple chapters in scripture and see he lived in a constant struggle between who he was and who God created him to be. There was a huge discrepancy between his choices and his calling. It seemed he ran into constant turmoil everywhere he went, not being able to make peace with anyone.

Struggles

When we leave one place in turmoil, we enter the next place already in trouble. Often God will send us back to the source of our struggle in order to overcome it. He'll send us back to forgive, ask forgiveness, find healing, or deal with shame. God will allow the past to haunt us until we address it and heal from it. When we leave a struggle with deep wounds, bitter feelings, stolen identity, and blame, we actually don't leave the struggle at all. It's entirely possible to leave the situation but keep the struggle.

So here we will find Jacob returning home to deal with his past and face his brother. What he refused to address was still there waiting for him.

Genesis 32:22-24 (NIV)

'That night Jacob got up and took his two wives, his two female servants and his eleven sons and crossed the ford of the Jabbok. After he had sent them across the stream, he sent over all his possessions. So Jacob was left alone, and a man wrestled with him till daybreak."

Interesting that Jacob sent away everything and every person he had and was left all alone. This was a place of desperation, you know the feeling. The moment when you throw up your hands and say, "I got nothing! There's nothing I can do but cry out to the Lord." There are many situations we face that are for God and God alone. There will be no satisfaction or relief from any person, relationship or possession that can bring the peace our souls must find. When we're left alone with God, there's only one outcome: *change*.

Genesis 32:25-26 (NIV)

"When the man saw that he could not overpower him, he touched the socket of Jacob's hip so that his hip was wrenched as he wrestled with the man. Then the man said, 'Let me go, for it is daybreak.'

But Jacob replied, 'I will not let you go unless you bless me.'"

Jacob wrestles with God the same way we do....and it hurt. We wrestle with what we want verses what we need. We wrestle with wanting to tune Him out because we don't feel like being there and would rather not learn any lesson He's trying to teach.

Struggle is about letting go of who we think we should be and embracing who we really are.

Before he goes to deal with the pain of his past, he has to face the God of his past. Behind every difficult situation is a God who loves us. If we don't tune into what He says in the worst of times, we're not likely to listen to Him in the best of times and we miss Him all together. Jacob finds out his real struggle isn't with Esau, it's within himself.

What controls us, consumes us. Jacob fought to control every situation he found himself in and was miserable.

Matthew 6:33 (NLT)

"Seek the Kingdom of God above all else, and live righteously, and he will give you everything you need."

Struggles

In every struggle, am I seeking God or am I self-seeking? Ouch. If we'll take our hands off, it makes room for Him to get a solid grip on it. We change the world when we fight for what's right and refuse to settle for what's easy.

My daughter was in gymnastics and came off the high bars with her hand all blistered, skin broken and in pain. She was up high when the bar started breaking her skin. She had two choices: let go and face the consequences or hold on, in pain, and learn a lesson.

The lesson: She should have chalked and taped her hand.

However, it healed quickly and the skin on her palms is becoming stronger each time. Her hands are forming from a girl who takes gymnastics classes to a girl who is a gymnast.

When we are able to hold onto God despite the pain when it feels easier to let go, we are handling ourselves not as one who goes to God, but as a child of God. We must first win the struggle within us to overcome the struggle around us.

There is no sin, misery, hurt, or dysfunction that God is not helping me through. In the middle of my fighting, I must pay close attention that I'm not fighting Jesus, but fighting for Him. Every struggle is a path to strength; a path that leads us to irrevocable truth.

You are called.
You are qualified.
You are accepted.
You are forgiven.
You are strong.

Jesus struggled with the cross all the way to Calvary to win those truths for us. He bled, sweat, was tortured, and carried his cross. There's nothing we can walk through that he can't relate to. Nothing. Without the struggle to the cross, there would be no salvation. Jesus' idea is simple: What doesn't defeat us, decreases us. Less of us and more of him.

Lord,

Thank You for struggles. Whether You put me in the middle of them or meet me in the middle of them, You always have a plan. Give me patience and help me to be steadfast, teaching me the lessons I need to learn along the way. Overflow my heart with joy knowing Your presence is with me always.

Day Thirty
Fear

Fear tells us to step down,
love tells us to step up.

As a mom, I spend a great amount of time answering "what if" questions. What if....*we run out of gas?* What if....*we get to school and it's cold inside?* What if....*your debit card runs out of money?* My favorite has been, "Mom, what if you stand up in front of everyone to teach and you fart?" Y'all. My kids seriously asked this.

The hypothetical is no friend of mine. What could happen and what should happen will drive us plumb crazy if we let it. Almost every single hesitation, followed by a "what if" question is bathed in worry and doubt. Why do we diagnose our every move through the worst case scenarios that play in our heads? Why do we spend precious time in fear of the unknown? Why do we rely on our own thoughts and not God's?

We fear being misunderstood, set aside, unappreciated and unimportant. And if we don't deal with this hideous emotion, when God calls us into action we will revert to our core fears:
What if I fail?

160

Bare Naked Truths

What if I get rejected?
What if I get hurt?

When my girls were much smaller, I used to walk them around one of the lakes in our neighborhood. I remember pushing one of my girls in her cute little red and blue car with a steering wheel that she could steer while the other was learning to ride her bike with training wheels. It was a beautiful day out. The sun was radiant, reflecting off the water and the clouds were puffy and white that day.

We were enjoying the day and strolling along, when out of nowhere came a huge pit bull that had clearly broken loose from the little boy who was walking him and chasing much, much farther behind. It didn't startle me until I realized that he had broken loose and was charging straight at us. He was face to face with my little girls and going straight for my youngest.

Momma bear sprung into action and I stepped away from my oldest to step in front of my youngest. When I did that, the dog changed his course and went for my older daughter instead. She panicked and became absolutely hysterical, jumping off her bike she began to run in circles and scream at the top of her tiny little lungs. Her hysteria sent me into a complete freak out moment. So I attempted to jump in front of her and the dog reverted back to my youngest. He was barking and had a plan to bite. In a last ditch effort, I charged the dog and screamed. The baby was crying, I was yelling and my oldest was still running in circles screaming. We were a sight!

The boy caught up with us, got the dog and walked off with a smirk on his face.

Fear has the ability to bring strong emotions out of us:
-panic

Fear

-rage
-resentment
-negativity
-frustration
-irritability
-impatience
-anxiety
-control

All of these emotions induce stress and toxic behavior. You know those people in your life who always walk around with negativity? It's probable that it's really just fear they are carrying.

Not only does it evoke a physical reaction, we also react spiritually to fear as well.

The things we fear the most can reveal where we trust God the least.

What kinds of things do you fear?

I used to fear what others might think about me. I would do whatever it took to gain the affirmation of others and would be devastated if it never came. One day I decided I was exhausted and worn out trying to make everyone happy. I asked the Lord to show me how to have peace in my life and He whispered this in my ear: *Kristin, you have to love pleasing me more than you love pleasing people. Rest in my love.*

"Perfect love casts out all fear" 1 John 4:18 (NIV).

Yes, perfect love does cast out all fear. I cling to that! It's also true that perfect *fear* casts out all *love*. When I choose to entertain my fears, I push away His love.

If we live with a spirit of fear, we live a lie. We can never be the person that God created us to be if we don't submit our fears to Him because we've cast out His perfect love.

Fear will back us down from our identity, our calling, our passions, and our purpose. It will tell us to sit down when it's time to rise up, to step down when love says to step up, and to cower in times that require courage. Fear is not something we were intended to operate out of. It's as if we are like little children, asking our Heavenly Father, "what if...your love isn't enough?"

If we spend all of our time worrying about the "what if's," we'll miss "what now's."

God doesn't call us to a comfort zone, He calls us out of one. I will be the first to tell you that the second you take your first step outside of it, you will stand face to face with fear.

The prophet Isaiah encourages us to forsake the thoughts that fear hurls at us.

"Let the wicked forsake their ways and the unrighteous their thoughts. Let them turn to the LORD, and he will have mercy on them, and to our God, for he will freely pardon" Isaiah 55:7 (NIV)

Fear

Forsake is a strong word, one that implies relation. In order to forsake something, you must have relied on it at some point. It was something you both claimed and maintained. You can't forsake something that never had a voice and place in your heart. But the good news, things are forsakable. You can call them forsaken. Forsook. Whatever. You get the point. It will require you to make a decision: Whose voice will you rely on? Where will you lend your ear and direct your thoughts?

You get to choose which "what if" statement you will ask. Can I give you some to think on?

What if....you can do all things through Christ who strengthens you (Philippians 4:13 NIV)

What if... you are a child of God (Galatians 3:26 NIV)

What if...you are equipped for the job?

(Romans 8:30 NIV)

What if....our God always causes us to triumph?

(2 Corinthians 2:14 NASB)

What if the very thing you are battling could unleash change in this world? What if...

Lord,

Show me what it means to truly allow Your perfect love into my heart. I want to see past the "what if's" in my life so I can see what You have for me. Thank you for the courage we have in You. Show me the areas that I'm fearing the most so that I can see where I trust You the least. I want You to have all of my heart.

Day Thirty One
Purpose

---

*You were made on purpose,
for a purpose.*

Genesis 1:28 (NIV)

"God blessed them and said to them, 'Be fruitful and increase in number; fill the earth and subdue it. Rule over the fish in the sea and the birds in the sky and over every living creature that moves on the ground.'"

The first words ever spoken to man held more weight than we could imagine. When God created man and woman, He knew He couldn't stop there, He's far too creative for that. He wanted to fill the earth with the beauty and life of His children.

When I had my first daughter, there was no agenda. Even from a young age, I always wanted a little girl to love and take care of. When God told us to "be fruitful and multiply," He knew that with every person born into this world came purpose. Purpose that was to be fruitful and purpose that was to be multiplied. I didn't have a child to fulfill selfish gain or to have an extra set of hands around the house. I didn't *need* her. I *wanted* her. I knew my husband and I had love in us and we desired to share it. Even as I carried her inside of me, I knew

Purpose

God had plans for her and that she could and would change the world.

Purpose is a tricky thing. We're all born with one and spend a lifetime trying to figure out what it is. It's often associated with what we are here to do. God doesn't sit up in heaven creating people so they can carry out tasks like worker bees. If that were the case, we hold too much power and run the risk of getting it all wrong and messing up God's perfect plan. We aren't that powerful. Our purpose isn't about us, it's about Him. In fact, what if our purpose could be defined in one word? Daughter. It's the starting point of who we are, the foundation on which we are built, the soil for which our roots develop, and the place where we go to find meaning.

We all want to make our lives count. We all want to be world changers. And we all want to live a life of purpose. Even though I repeatedly fail God, He has never failed me, *not once*. When I place my value in what I do, it's never enough and I feel like a constant failure. What a silly girl I am thinking that His plans are contingent on my actions or inactions.

When we are hired on at a company, we must know our role before we can do our job. How often have you seen someone dismissed from their work because they either weren't doing their job or took it upon themselves to do someone else's? The same philosophy is true of the body of Christ. We must know our job description before we can be effective at the work. *Before we are anything, we are His. We are His children.* Being a child means we must allow God to raise us. It's not enough to just be created by Him, we must accept Him as our Father.

Exodus 9:16 (NIV)

"But I have raised you up for this very purpose, that I might show you my power and that my name might be proclaimed in all the earth."

God continually shows us His power, but we must look for it. The older we get, the more we can look back and collect lessons with each memory- good or bad. *What we live presently is always linked to what we've lived previously.* In order to accept myself as a daughter of the King, I must view Him as a Father; one that is present and engaged. He's the kind of Father that has been there all along, always desiring to speak to us. Like a good Father, He wants us to glean from past experiences. It's a powerful thing to look back and intentionally celebrate what God has done for us, the lessons He's taught, the things He's set us free from, and the truth He managed to deposit deep in our hearts. I don't want to get so busy doing things for the Lord that I miss what the Lord has done for me.

We are all a work in progress. Part of being raised up by the Lord for purpose is to recognize what He's placed in us. Whether we realize it or not, our passions point us to our purpose. They are God given and are there for a reason. It's what we're made to do or do something about.

Take Action.

List out your passions: What do you love and love to do? What sparks a fire in you? What makes you angry?

If you could do anything, what would it be? What do you absolutely have to talk about?

Establish your Core Beliefs: (hint, this is done in prayer with the Holy Spirit). Core Beliefs are your governing life principles. They both define who you are and set the guardrails to how you live out your identity. Ask the Lord to show you the unique things He's placed in you and the things He has said are true about you. Examine your greatest struggles and victories and how those things shaped you into the person you are today. I have mine written in the front of my Bible and refer to them often. It's how I process, filter, and make decisions in life.

Gather your Favorite Scriptures: God draws *your* heart to HIS words for a specific reason. He places them *in* you so that He can tell His story *through* you. Make a list of your favorite scriptures and ask the Lord to show you the common denominator.

When I begin to see Him in me, I begin to see me in Him.

There really isn't any pressure in our purpose. Oh, how we get ahead of God! We rush into His promises and freedom like we know the way and don't need any further instruction. All the while, He is willing to answer our prayers when we ask Him for direction and clarity. Life is too precious of a gift to give it our best guess or make decisions based on what feels right. We must spend time getting our instructions from the Lord and not our gut.

Psalm 37:23 (NIV)
"The LORD directs the steps of the godly. He delights in every detail of their lives."

Purpose means I don't live in a way where the world sees me, I live in a way where they see Him.

You were made for greatness. Let's commit to only chase after the assignments the Lord gives us, not anything else. Let's spend time with Him so that we develop the 'Jesus desires' inside of us rather than our own desires. Let's feed the relationships that God ordains and be very purposeful about where we invest our time, interests, and heart. Let's spend our days and years putting God on the throne of our hearts so that the things that flow from it are ruled by Him.

Lord,

I want my life to honor You: past, present, and future. Take everything in my life and use it for Your purpose. Reveal what You've placed inside of me and show me how to serve others with that. Show me how to be content to be Your daughter before I'm anything else. With you by my side, I will not fail.

Bare Naked Challenge

Thank you for spending the last 31 days intentionally embracing the truth that sets you free. I pray it has sunk deeply into your soul and done your heart good. If you're anything like me, as you were reading, God was downloading your own thoughts and experiences and re-writing history. My fervent prayers are that through this time in scripture, God has thumped you on the head to reveal a sneaky little lie that has made its way into what you believe. From now on when you feel it trying to creep its way back in, you can strip it off like wax to an unwanted hair.

Part of our destiny as Christ followers is not leaving people the way we found them. Offering a kind word, a gentle smile, compassion, and genuinely caring is what we are called to.

As time with Jesus sets us free, we must share freedom with others. Free people, free people. Here is our challenge to be a truth teller:

Listen carefully to others as they speak. When you hear them speaking untruth, call them out. We must be the kind of friends that won't allow a false belief. Don't be afraid to be the friend that says, "You've believed a lie." Be a truth girl. We can't remain silent, it's too costly. You know the truth, now tell it!

Endnotes

Endnotes

Day 4:
The Man in the Arena, Theodore Roosevelt
Excerpt from the speech "Citizenship In A Republic" delivered at the Sorbonne, in Paris, France on 23 April, 1910

Day 6:
Facing the Giants. Alex Kendrick. Sherwood Pictures, 2006 Film.

Day 12:
Suzanne Eller, Proverbs 31 Ministries. (n.d.). Retrieved January 31, 2017, from http://tsuzanneeller.com/

Day 13:
Smedes, L. B. (1984). Forgive and forget: healing the hurts we don't deserve. San Francisco: Harper & Row.

Day 19:
World War I Christmas Truce. (2014, November 18). Retrieved January 31, 2017, from
http://www.snopes.com/holidays/christmas/truce.asp

Silk, D. (2008). Loving our kids on purpose: making a heart-to-heart connection. Shippensburg, PA: Destiny Image Pubs., Inc.

Day 21:
Allen, J. (n.d.). God Doesn't Need You to Try So Hard. Retrieved January 31, 2017, from

http://www.christianitytoday.com/women/2017/january/god-doesnt-need-you-to-try-so-hard.html

H. (2010, February 16). How I Almost Quit. Retrieved January 31, 2017, from http://www.desiringgod.org/articles/how-i-almost-quit

Day 22:
(n.d.). Retrieved January 31, 2017, from https://www.merriam-webster.com/

Day 24:
Prison was Mandela's greatest teacher. (2010, March 29). Retrieved January 31, 2017, from http://www.today.com/popculture/prison-was-mandela-s-greatest-teacher-wbna36087300

Day 25:
Brown, B. (2010). The gifts of imperfection: let go of who you think you're supposed to be and embrace who you are. Center City, MN: Hazelden.

Day 26:
Skeat, Walter W., and C. S. Lewis. A concise etymological dictionary of the English language, by the Rev. Walter W. Skeat .. Oxford: Clarendon Press, 1911. Print.

Spurgeon, C. H., and Daniel Partner. The essential works of Charles Spurgeon: selected books, sermons, and other writings ... Uhrichsville, OH: Barbour Pub., 2009. Print.

CPSIA information can be obtained
at www.ICGtesting.com
Printed in the USA
FFOW05n1518171017